Anna Schrade

A JOURNEY
THROUGH
EUROPE

Societies, politics, and contemporary issues in the EU

Kwansei Gakuin University Press

Anna Schrade is Associate Professor at the Institute for Industrial Research, Kwansei Gakuin University, Japan, where she has been teaching EU politics and economics since 2018. Prior, she was Associate Professor at Kobe University, in charge of their newly established Programme for European Studies.

She holds an MA in European Studies from the University of Bath/ Institut d'Études Politiques de Paris (Sciences Po), as well as an MSc in Japanese Studies and a PhD in History, both from the University of Oxford. Her main expertise is comparative EU-Japanese politics, with special focus on rural development and labour migration, and she has published widely on these topics.

Between 2019 and 2022, under Dr Schrade's lead, Kwansei Gakuin University was awarded the prestigious Jean Monnet Module by the European Commission.

A journey through Europe:
Societies, politics, and contemporary issues in the EU

Kwansei Gakuin University Press
1-1-155 Uegahara, Nishinomiya, Hyogo, 662-0891, Japan
ISBN: 978-4-86283-343-3

The European Commission's support for the production of this publication does not constitute an endorsement of the contents, which reflect the views only of the authors, and the Commission cannot be held responsible for any use which may be made of the information contained therein.

CONTENTS

V GREECE: 129

Greece and the Eurozone crisis: what are the reasons behind Greece's downfall, and why is the economy only recovering slowly?

VI ITALY: 165

The rise of the Mummy's Boys (*mammoni*): why do so many Italian live with their parents?

Fig. 1 Map of Europe

Countries discussed in this book are highlighted in grey.

Introduction

Europe: a continent of dichotomies and contradictions, but also a continent of innovation, outstanding social activism, and exemplary soft power. What makes Europe special? What are some of the most urgent social, political, and economic issues European countries are currently grappling with? What are their approaches, and what can we learn from Europe?

This book invites the interested reader–whether scholars, students, policymakers, or the general public–to get to know more about contemporary European countries, with all their challenges and political issues. As Europe is too big and too diverse (or even contradictory) to make sense of as a whole, we have picked six countries to provide a range of insights into some of the big socio-economic issues EU member states face. Topics range from Polish and Romanian labour mobility to the UK, refugees in Germany, female labour force participation and gender equality in Sweden, Italy's slack labour market and the rise of 'mammoni' (mummy's boys), Greece's structural problems that have slowed down economic recovery after the country's sovereign debt crisis, and the rural-urban divide in Romania, which has triggered massive internal and external migration over the past decades.

According to the EU's motto 'United in Diversity', this book hopes to display some of the many aspects of European societies, economics, and politics. Considering it only sheds light on some of the most pressing questions students might have, we have chosen *A Journey Through Europe* as its title. The idea behind this concept is that the authors–Anna Schrade and Andrei Herinean, who co-authored Chapter IV on Romania–take the reader on an imaginary tour through Europe by discussing some of the most puzzling phenomena in different countries. This way, readers learn about the history, culture, politics, economics, and society of several EU member states and understand what life is like in different countries within this economic (and geographic) bloc.

Each of the six chapters tries to answer one major question (or puzzle) that makes the country special and thus an interesting case to study. In the first chapter, we will focus on Sweden, not only trying to understand why the country has an extremely high female employment rate, with nearly as many women as men part of the workforce, but why motherhood is positively correlated with employment. Under the title 'Women at work: why do so many Swedish mothers work?' Chapter I assesses how it is possible that a whopping 85% of mothers with two children under 14 are gainfully employed. We will reveal that the secrets behind Sweden's high female employment rate are decades of investment inand promotion ofgender equality, as well as the country's tight net of childcare services and institutional support for working mothers. Sweden's high degree of gender equality not only translates into a large share of fathers taking parental leave, which allows some mothers to return to work relatively early after childbirth, but also entails flexible working arrangements for women, including flex-time options, remote work, part-time positions, and generous sick childcare leave. With men and women sharing household chores and child-rearing duties more equally than in many other countries, and with daycare facilities for babies and toddlers being universally available (sometimes even 24/7), Swedish mothers have the time, flexibility, and support to engage in paid work, resulting in only about one in seven mothers aged 20 to 64 with small children not being part of the labour force.

In Chapter II, we move from Sweden to the UK. Although the UK is an island, it is possible to drive from Sweden's capital, Stockholm, to London–crossing the Channel either by ferry or using the modern tunnel system that connects France's Calais with Dover, a city in the southeast of England. If one were to drive from Sweden to England, one would spend about 27 hours in the car to make the 2,500 km long journey, crossing through Denmark, Germany, the Netherlands, Belgium, and France. We selected the UK as our second case study because of its high share of citizens from the EU's eastern states. While at the time of the EU's Eastern Enlargement in 2004, less than 70,000 Poles lived in the UK, the Polish community in Britain surpassed one million in 2017. The rise of Romanian residents is equally impressive, from around 17,000 in 2006, the year before Romania joined the EU, to 427,000 in 2019. Our lead question (and title) is thus: "Coming to work: why have so many (young) people from Poland and Romania moved to the UK?"

In order to understand the decision of hundreds of thousands of (young) Poles and Romanians to move to the UK, we analyse the push factors that have driven the emigrants to leave their home country, such as unemployment, low wages, limited career opportunities, a lack of social welfare and dissatisfaction with the political system at home, to name just a few. In addition, we assess the pull factors that have attracted workers from the EU's new member states to move to Britain since 2004. The chapter highlights that, while social and political reasons played an important role, many emigrants were largely motivated by financial reasons. In the early years after the EU's eastern enlargement, the wage gaps between the UK and the new member states were so significant–with many new residents from Poland and Romania being able to make more money in the UK in two months than they would at home in a whole year–that thousands of Poles and Romanians even left behind classically 'desirable' jobs in favour of physical or unskilled labour in the UK (as they were handsomely rewarded for this).

Chapter III takes us from the UK to Germany, another country where a high number of Polish and Romanian nationals reside. While this chapter also looks at migration, its focus is not on labour migration, but on refugees from Syria and Iraq. In contrast to the many Romanians and Poles who moved to the UK for work reasons, the hundreds of thousands of Syrians and Iraqis who have reached Germany since 2015 did so to find a safe haven from civil war and terrorism. The reason why we chose Germany as our case study is because of the huge number of refugees the country has taken in since 2015: out of the roughly one million Syrians refugees that arrived in the EU between 2011 and 2017, half of them found asylum in Germany.

Under the title "Why does Germany have so many refugees from the Middle East?" Chapter III tries to reveal why hundreds of thousands refugees from Syria and Iraq chose Germany as their destination. It analyses some of the political, social, and economic reasons and historical explanations for Germany granting asylum to the vast majority of applicants from Syria and Iraq. We show that Germany was attractive for many asylum seekers from the Middle East because they were often more familiar with the country than with other EU nations (which also includes having friends and relatives there) and because Germany's support system for asylum seekers is one of the most generous in the bloc. In addition, Germany's high asylum recognition rate, especially in 2015, when nearly all applicants from Syria and Iraq received a positive result on their application, increased many refugees' desire to apply for asylum there in order to maximise their chances of remaining in Europe legally for longer.

In Chapter IV, our journey takes us to southeast Europe. We 'visit' Romania, one of the EU's newest member states. At the time of writing, Romania has been an EU member state for 15 years. Despite Romania's rapid economic development in the wake of its accession, the country remains one of the poorest in the EU. Many rural areas in particular have been left out of the country's recent economic and social progress. Under the title "Looking for a better life abroad or in the city: why have so many Romanians left the countryside", the two authors, Andrei Herinean and Anna Schrade, asses the many reasons why Romanians moved away from the countryside in droves. They highlight that rising social inequalities, such as the income inequality between rural and urban populations, poor medical services and often desolate schools, as well as a general lack of proper infrastructure (e.g. roads, trains or sanitary systems) in many rural villages have driven hundreds of thousands to urban or suburban areas. In addition, over a million Romanians have left for other EU member states since the country's EU accession in 2007 (as discussed in Chapter II). While the many remittances Romanians have sent from their new country of residence (such as the UK or Germany) to their families staying behind in the Romanian countryside have greatly contributed to the development of Romania's rural areas and have improved the quality of life there, internal and external migration has also contributed to the 'greying' (or even complete disappearance) of many Romanian villages.

In Chapter V, our journey continues to Greece, a country around half the size of Romania in terms of population. Although Greece has been an EU member state since 1981, only in 2007, with the accession of Bulgaria and Romania, did Greece start to share a border with another EU member state (namely Bulgaria, which is located to the north of Greece). Despite the geographical proximity–driving from Romania's capital Bucharest to Greece's Thessaloniki takes a mere eight hours–life in Romania and Greece is all but similar, not only because of the different cultural and ethnic backgrounds but also because of the countries' distinct histories and the long communist rule in Romania. Yet, the countries also have several commonalities, such as structural economic problems and social inequality. As discussed in Chapter IV, much of Romania's countryside suffers from a lack of financial resources and good governance. In Greece, similarly, the government's budget has been under tight control since the country entered a severe government debt crisis that followed the Global Financial Crisis (2007–2009). Under the title "Greece and the Eurozone crisis: what are the reasons behind Greece's downfall, and why is the economy only recovering slowly?" this chapter analyses the reasons behind Greece's economic decline, which has reduced the country's GDP by over 25% between 2008 and 2014 and which has led to the biggest financial bailout in history, as Greece had to borrow €320 billion to avert bankruptcy.

This chapter looks at the structural reasons behind Greece's long recession (2008–2016), rampant unemployment, and Europe's highest GDP-to-debt ratio. It reveals that the main factors for Greece's economic decline were not the euro and the EU's financial system, but deep-rooted structural problems such as the country's low employment rate, options for early retirement with relatively generous pensions, rampant corruption and a sizeable shadow economy, and the rising trade deficit due to an increasing lack of competitiveness among many of Greece's businesses.

For Chapter VI, we cross the Mediterranean Sea to reach Italy. Although Greece's Corfu is located less than 200 kilometres east of Italy's province Apulia, the ferry from Brindisi to Corfu takes eight hours. Cultural and economic exchange between Greece and Italy is widespread, not only because both countries have been EU member states for over 40 years, but also because Greece and Italy, as two Mediterranean countries, share considerable cultural and culinary similarities. Some of these parallels are visible in the countries' labour markets: both suffer from a high unemployment rate, especially among the youth, and a low representation of women in the labour market. Under the title "The rise of the Mummy's Boys (*mammoni*): why do so many young Italian men live with their parents?" Chapter VI assesses how Italy's high youth unemployment contributes to the late departure of many Italian sons from the parental home. While in northern European countries, the majority of youngsters gain residential independency after secondary school or in their early 20s, Italian men, on average, only leave the parental home after their 30th birthday. With three quarters of all young males between 18 and 34 residing in the family home, cohabitation between parents and their adult sons has become so common that a new term was coined: *mammone* (plural: *mammoni*), or mummy's boy (s). This chapter looks at the cultural, economic, and social reasons for the late departure from the parental home. It highlights that, in addition to a lack of financial stability due to high youth unemployment, precarious work conditions, temporary contracts and low salaries also prevalent among many entry-level Italian workers, there is poor availability of small, reasonably priced housing in many of Italy's cities. Combined, these factors led to the (unsurprising) rise of *mammoni*. Yet, also cultural norms and traditions, such as many mothers' desire to care for their sons well into adulthood and the preference among many young men to reside at home and enjoy the comforts of *Hotel Mamma*, play important roles.

Although the focus of the six chapters is extremely diverse, several parallels exist. While, for example, Chapter II analyses why so many Romanian workers moved to the UK, Chapter IV provides more information on the push factors that have driven Romanians to leave the countryside and to move to bigger cities, both at home or abroad. It provides further insights into the living conditions among rural Romanian dwellers, which explain why hundreds of thousands of them have chosen to move to the UK in search for higher living standards and new career chances.

Similarly, Chapter II and III form a synthesis, as they both look at pull factors that have attracted work migrants and refugees to the UK and Germany, respectively. Also, Chapter V and VI are related, as the labour market and high (youth) unemployment play a central role in explaining why the Greek economy was hit so hard since 2008 and for understanding the high prevalence of cohabitation between parents and their adult sons in Italy. Chapter I also assesses employment, but it provides an example of how a well-functioning labour market and high levels of gender equality not only boost Sweden's female employment rate but also spur economic growth– something that is missing in Italy and Greece.

What connects all the chapters is the fact that they all deal with 'big questions.' This is one of the novelties of this book, and a point that makes it appealing to a wide range of readers. Instead of trying to make sense of Europe as a whole or to explain policymaking in the EU, this publication hopes to increase readers' understanding of Europe by shedding new light on the recent 'big' developments in different European countries. By selecting some of the most puzzling questions, the authors hope to motivate people of all ages, around the world, to study European issues.

SWEDEN:

I

Women at work: why do so many Swedish mothers work?

Abstract   OECD countries have been striving to increase their female labour force participation for decades, yet not all have been successful. While southern European countries, such as Italy and Greece, still have low employment rates for women, the Scandinavian countries, above all Sweden, have managed to nearly close the gender employment gap. Having surpassed a female employment rate of 80% among 20–64-year-olds in most years since the 1980s, Sweden has achieved a high degree of gender equality in employment. What is more, motherhood is positively correlated with employment: for women with one or two children under 14, the employment rate is a whopping 85%. This is because of a high degree of gender equality at work and at home, generous parental leave policies for women and men–with both sexes taking a large share of their leave–universally-available childcare, social norms and policies that support dual income families, as well as flexible work arrangements such as flextime, remote work, and part-time options.

What this chapter covers: Gender equality, Nordic welfare state, family policies, policies promoting female employment, labour market conditions, childcare, household chores, new work styles

Introduction

Swedish women can have it all–that is the impression many Europeans have of the Scandinavian country that ranks No. 1 in the EU in terms of gender equality (IEIGE, 2021). While southern EU member states have had considerable problems raising both fertility rates and female labour force participation, Sweden managed to have a fertility rate averaging over 1.8 children per couple over the past decade. At the same time, the female labour force participation rate among women aged 15 to 64 was 81.2% (2019), a figure only marginally below that of Swedish men (World Bank, 2021). Surprisingly, the female employment rate among women with children aged 0–14 is even higher, surpassing 85%–with the vast majority (77%) working full time (OECD, 2020).

Yet, it is not only the fact that so many Swedish women work that makes the country interesting for social scientists, economists, and gender specialists; the high representation of women in responsible and highly regarded positions such as doctors, professors, politicians, and managers also makes Sweden an interesting country to study. How can Swedish women combine having kids with a career? What enables the country to have such a high female employment rate?

This chapter investigates possible reasons for the significant labour force participation among Swedish women by analysing welfare state policies that support families and enable women to work. By looking at childcare arrangements, maternity and parental leave provisions, family policies and flexible work arrangements, this chapter reveals that the Swedish welfare state with its strong focus on (gender) equality has laid a sound foundation for female employment. In addition, we show that the flexibility of many Swedish companies regarding flextime, remote work and reduced working hours, as well as a high share of public employment, enables Swedish women to work at a much higher degree than in most other EU countries.

In the following, we investigate how different social policies, the high prevalence of gender equality, Swedish norms, culture and history, and the flexibility of the Swedish labour market in terms of working arrangements impact employment and the fertility rate among Swedes.

While Sweden's Nordic neighbours (Finland, Denmark, Norway, and Iceland) also have relatively high fertility and high female employment, Sweden's performance remains unmatched.

Female employment and motherhood in Sweden

When comparing female labour force participation in Sweden and Japan, two points are salient: the generally much higher labour force participation of women and the absence of an M-curve (with female employment taking a dip when most women marry or have children, only bouncing back around 15 years later) in Sweden. In Japan, women historically left the workforce once they married–the few years of work experience between graduation and married life were often referred to as *koshikake*, or 'sitting down temporarily.' In Sweden, however, female labour force participation not only remains relatively constant during women's 30s and 40s but increases in their 30s–a time when most women have small children. Back in Japan, female employment for women in their late 20s is considerably higher than in their 30s, while the reverse is true for Sweden (OECD, 2022c). Indeed, Sweden is one of the few countries where motherhood is positively correlated with employment, which means that women with children have a higher employment rate than their childless counterparts. The difference among these groups is a striking 10% in favour of women with children. In most other EU member states, motherhood has a negative impact on female employment–in Hungary, for example, the difference in employment between mothers and childless women was as stark as 36% in 2015, and in the UK and Germany, motherhood translated into a 17% and 15% lower employment rate (European Commission, 2017).

Why is it the case that the Swedish female employment rate rises at a time when most of them give birth and raise small children, and that the labour force participation of mothers is higher than that of childless women? In the following, we analyse several socio-economic policies targeting families and employment that increase the labour force participation rate among Swedish women, especially mothers, such as formal childcare, parental leave policies, public employment, and flexible work conditions. The analysis shows that the general availability of cheap, high-quality childcare from an early age, generous leave policies for both mothers and fathers that are valid until the child turns eight, flexible work arrangements and the possibility to work from home several hours a week (guaranteed by law), a high involvement of fathers in childrearing and household chores, as well as the Swedish mentality and strong welfare state that supports and promotes the dual earner model all play a major role for Sweden's high female employment rate.

Why do so many Swedish women work?

1) Cultural and historical reasons

Until the second half of the 19th century, most Swedish women were not gainfully employed, but worked at home, looking after the children, managing the household, and supporting the husband's farming activities. When industrialisation started to spread in Sweden in the late 19th century, people increasingly moved to the cities to seek employment in the growing number of factories. Poor women, widows and single mothers in particular became increasingly engaged in factory work (Nordic Council of Ministers, 2006). While the employment rate of working-age women fluctuated around 30% between 1925 and 1965, the 1970s and 80s witnessed a major spike in female employment, with the result that, by 1982, over 83% of Swedish married women aged 20–59 were employed (Gustafsson/ Jacobsson, 1985). Data from the 1980s reveal that Sweden quickly assumed its leading role in regard to female employment and gender equality, with its female labour force participation rate being about twice as high as in Italy and Japan. While over 83% of all women aged 35–54 were gainfully employed in Sweden in 1980, Japanese statistics reveal a dismal 30%. What is also interesting is that, in 1980, Sweden's female labour force participation rate did not drop when women reached child-bearing age (25–34) but increased–a development considerably different from its European neighbours, the US, and Japan (Gustafsson/Jacobsson, 1985). This leads us to the question as to how Sweden managed to become a pioneer in female employment already by the second half of the 20th century.

The main reason lies within the Swedish universal welfare state model with its strong focus on (gender) equality and the subsequent provision of generous policies regarding family, maternity leave, and childcare. While the foundations for Sweden's welfare state were laid already in the early 20th century, including the laws to support working mothers, the immediate post-war period (1946–50) can be considered the cradle of the Swedish universal welfare state. These years, which are often referred to as the 'great period of reform', saw comprehensive new laws on child allowances, old-age pensions, health insurance and education, which allowed more women to receive tertiary education and to combine family and work (Nordic Council of Ministers, 2006). While maternity and parental leave polices had been in place since the 1930s, the mid-1970s witnessed a major reform of the system, with more generous leave policies and larger financial provisions, as well as greater gender equality even in child-rearing (with Swedish fathers being able to take substantial amounts of childcare leave since 1974). All these policies allowed women more flexibility regarding work and enabled them to remain in gainful employment even after childbirth.

Yet it is not only the pull side (the factors making work more attractive for women, such as higher demand for workers and more generous family policies) that led to the rise in female employment in the 1960s and 70s. The universal welfare state also had a considerable impact on Swedish women's mindset and the new social 'norm' that all people, whether male or female, should become part of the labour force. From the very beginning, it was clear for both politicians and the general population that generous welfare provisions, as introduced after 1946, were only sustainable long-term if the large majority of the Swedish population was gainfully employed, thereby financing social welfare provisions through their income tax contributions and the corporate tax payments by their employers, among others. Unlike in countries such as Germany, Belgium, or Austria, which largely implemented a Bismarck-style corporatist welfare state where men remained the major breadwinners for decades, the Nordic universal welfare state model encouraged universal employment and incentivised female labour force participation. In many central and southern European countries, female employment among women with small children was largely frowned upon, with many conservative politicians propagating that children should be raised by their mothers and not by institutionalised care facilities at least until the 1990s. However, the Nordic countries had a much more modern and liberal approach to female employment (Nordic Council of Ministers, 2019a). Indeed, most parts of Swedish society were well aware that having women return to work within one year of childbirth would increase the wealth of the country and would keep the welfare state alive. Thus, it can be argued that Sweden's modern history, its socialist traditions with a strong focus on universal employment and generous welfare policies covering the whole population, as well as the Swedish mentality of formalised childcare being valuable for children, families, employers, and society at large, has played a major role for mothers' high labour force participation.

Examples from other EU member states reveals similar tendencies regarding how the history of female employment, social norms and the mindset among women impacts women's labour force participation. In some of the formerly communist eastern EU member states, female labour force participation is extremely high, with all three Baltic countries (Lithuania, Estonia, and Latvia) surpassing Denmark and Finland in regard to female labour force participation (Eurostat, 2020). This stems from the communist ideology that everyone–including women–had to contribute to society by being part of the workforce and confirms the role history and social norms play in regard to female employment.

2) Social welfare policies: childcare provisions

One of the biggest factors impacting the labour force participation of mothers is the provision of childcare facilities. In countries where formal state-supported childcare for kids under three have been the norm for decades, such as in the Nordic countries, the Netherlands, France, Luxembourg and Eastern Germany, women tend to have a relatively high labour force participation. It goes without saying that the labour market conditions also play an enormous role in female employment and that an abundance of childcare facilities does not necessarily guarantee high female employment. Yet, assessing the availability of formalised childcare for children Under three, there is a strong positive correlation between the availability of nurseries and female employment. Most of the 11 EU member states[1] that have reached or surpassed the Barcelona targets for high-quality, affordable childcare–set at 33% of all children from 0 to 3 in formal care arrangements–have relatively high labour force participation (European Commission, 2018). Out of the 11 countries, only three–Italy, Spain and Belgium–had a female labour force participation rate below 70% for all women aged 20 to 64 (Eurostat, 2020). The reasons for these outliers could be the low availability of jobs due to a slack labour market and the short history of childcare for under three-year-olds (in Italy, for example, just over 20% of all children below the age three were in formal childcare in 2013).

There is consensus that a lack of adequate formal childcare can, but does not necessarily have to, negatively impact female employment. A good example of the exception are the Baltic states Lithuania and Latvia, where female employment is among the highest in the EU although just 15% of under three-year-olds attend formal nurseries in Lithuania, and 28% in Latvia (European Commission, 2018). Yet, in Japan, insufficient childcare facilities, especially in the big cities, contribute to the relatively low female labour force participation rate. According to the OECD, "childcare

---

[1] Namely Denmark, Netherlands, Sweden, Luxembourg, Portugal Belgium, Slovenia, France, Spain, and Germany.

shortages in some urban areas" are one of the reasons why female employment in Japan has not yet reached its full potential (OECD, 2017).

In Sweden, reasonably priced, high-quality formalised childcare has been universally available since the 1980s, with the result that nowadays, Sweden has one of the best, cheapest and most flexible childcare arrangements not only in the EU, but also globally. From the year the child turns one, Swedish babies can attend nursery (called *Förskol*, or preschools). Most children attend preschool until they enter primary school aged six, staying at the same facilities for several years. To accommodate the parents' different working schedules, public (communal) preschools usually start at 6:00 am and remain open until 18:30–for a whole 12-and-a-half hours! Some private preschools even offer round-the-clock childcare, accommodating parents who work irregular hours or nighttime shifts.

In principle, all children under primary school age can be offered a spot in a childcare facility, without waiting lists (Nordic Council of Ministers, 2019b). As a result, the large majority of Swedish children are taken care of in formal institutions, with around 97% of all children aged three to six attending kindergarten, and over 50% of under three-year-olds enrolled in a nursery in 2016 (European Commission, 2018). Those parents who choose not to send their child to nursery or kindergarten (in Sweden, both types are called preschool) mainly do this for personal reasons and not because of a lack of facilities or high costs. In fact, as nurseries do not cost more than SEK 1,382 (a mere €132) per child (with lower fees for low-income families and subsequent kids, and free care from the fourth child onwards), financial reasons play a marginal role in parents choosing to care for their children at home. In fact, only 0.7% of all parents not having their pre-school children in formalised care do so for financial reasons–the lowest figure in the EU, and substantially below the EU average of 16.2% (Nordic Council of Ministers, 2019b). A lack of nursery spots is not an issue, either, with only 1.2% of all parents with preschool children outside formalised childcare mentioning that it was a major factor. Similarly, as opening hours are very flexible, with some nurseries being open 24 hours a day, a lack of suitable working hours is also not a major hindrance (1.8% of all mentions in the survey). The general satisfaction with Swedish childcare facilities is best displayed by the fact that even among those who opted not to send their children to institutionalised care, a mere 0.1% stated that they believe the quality is not good (Nordic Council of Ministers, 2019b).

Swedish childcare stands out for its very reasonable price. Both private and public preschools have the same fee structure, with the (maximum) fees set by the government. For one child, the monthly costs are SEK 1,382 (€132), or 3% of the parents' gross income, whatever is lower. The fees for the second child are reduced by one third (costing SEK 922/€88 or a maximum of 2% of the gross income), while the third child can attend preschool for as little as SEK 451/€44 or 1% of the gross income, whichever is lower). From child number four, preschool education is free (European Commission, 2021).

To guarantee the high quality of Swedish preschools and to make sure all children have attained certain skills by the time they enter primary school, the state sets a standard curriculum that all preschools, public and private, follow. The high rate of children in preschool and the state's strict supervision and guidance guarantee that all Swedish kids have similar skills by the time they reach school age, which reduces inequality and allows for a smooth transition from preschool to primary school. Another way of guaranteeing high quality is teachers' education. Unlike in most other countries, Swedish preschool teachers and pedagogues (even those in charge of leisure time activities) must have a three-to-four-year tertiary degree. Even child assistants, who have a supporting role, tend to have a professional three-year tertiary diploma. The high degree of education and training is reflected in the fact that, in 2006, "almost all (98%) staff in Swedish preschool centres [were] trained to work with children", according to OECD data (OECD, 2006). In addition, while not required by law, many preschool educators engage in lifelong learning and receive further education and training after several years of work experience, for which state grants are available.

Swedish preschools have been an important tool for lifting Sweden's female labour force participation. The large number of preschools, which guarantee relatively quick and easy access for all children, the high degree of flexibility with long opening hours, high quality of education according to state-set, national curriculums, and good education and training of teachers make Swedish preschools a top choice for many mothers. The high level of trust in public and private childcare institutions and the ease of finding a suitable nursery allow mothers to place their children in formal care from an early age onwards. Thus, it can be concluded that Sweden's high-quality institutionalised childcare system plays a major role in allowing women with young children to work, positively impacting the country's female employment rate.

3) Generous leave policies

Leave policies are an effective tool for integrating women into the labour market after childbirth and child-raising. While there is no consensus regarding the ideal length of parental leave for men and women, Sweden's maternity and childcare leave policies are considered another major factor that explains the country's high employment rate among mothers.

Sweden is not only the country with the oldest maternity leave policies, which date back to 1900, but it also has one of the most generous parental leave regulations for both mothers and fathers. In fact, Sweden was the first country to make parental leave more gender-neutral, allowing fathers to take a large share of the parental leave as far back as 1974. With fathers being able to spend considerable time off work, the uptake of leave months by fathers is among the highest in Sweden, which also contributes to women being able to return to work relatively quickly after childbirth (European Commission, 2018).

When Swedish women first received financial compensation during maternity leave (no matter if they were gainfully employed or not before childbirth) in 1955–nearly 70 years ago–the new law only covered 12 weeks, during which the mother could stay at home while receiving financial support from the government. Since then, both the length and the amount paid have been considerably extended so that today, Swedish parents get a whopping 480 days of maternity and childcare leave to be split among the mother and father. To encourage fathers to have a leave of absence to care for their child, 90 out of these 480 days are reserved solely for the father. In other words, couples can only receive compensation for up to 480 days if the father takes at least 90 days off work. Of course, fathers can take more than just 90 days. In fact, it would theoretically be possible for fathers to take 390 days of parental leave, with the mother returning to work soon after maternity leave.

The long history of parental leave provisions for men, the Swedish mentality that supports gender equality and dual earner households, as well as the high degree of flexibility–fathers and mothers can take leave simultaneously, leave work only for some hours per week, take their leave up to when the child turns eight, or can work part-time while on leave–has increased the share of leave taken by fathers (Nordic Council of Ministers, 2019a). Sweden currently has one of the highest uptake rates of parental leave among fathers, with around 90% of Swedish fathers taking time off after childbirth. In 2017, 28% of parental leave days were taken by fathers, according to annual statistics by the Swedish Social Insurance Agency–a figure considerably higher than in other EU or OECD countries (Duvander/Löfgren, 2019).

Swedish parental leave arrangements are not only generous in length, but also in terms of financial compensation. For 390 days, parents can receive up to 80% of the average salary they received in the 12 months prior to childbirth (in the case of public sector employees, part of the parental leave benefits can cover as much as 100% of their previous salary). However, to prevent public finances from skyrocketing, there is a ceiling regarding the maximum childcare benefits: above a certain threshold of income, childcare allowances do not increase anymore, but are capped at SEK 1,021 (€97) per day. The remaining 90 days are paid at a flat rate of SEK 180 (€19) per day (European Commission, n.d.). In contrast to Japan, mothers or fathers who were not gainfully employed before childbirth are also entitled to paid parental leave.

Yet, it is not only the rising financial compensation that has increased the number of mothers and fathers taking paid leave. Another important factor is the flexibility that comes with parental leave. Since 1976, parents were given the right to work part-time during their leave. This potentially means that they do not leave the labour market completely but remain in close contact with their employer or their colleagues and keep their skills and knowledge updated. The rationale behind this provision is that being completely out of the workforce for a certain time could reduce the likelihood that people return to work after their leave, as they might have lost touch with the employment world. Skills and knowledge could become lost or outdated after a certain time, and lack of connection could mean that employees on leave are less eager to return to work when the time comes. Working part-time during childcare leave could also show the parent's dedication and fitness for work and reduce the occurrence of maternity harassment, which is relatively common in Japan. In fact, the lack of flexibility and the lack of opportunities for regular part-time employment during parental leave in Japan could be a major reason why most mothers do not return to the workforce after childbirth but stay at home with the child until it reaches secondary school.

Even when the 480 days of childcare leave are over, Swedish parents have the right to reduce their regular working hours by 25% until the child's eighth birthday (of course, only the hours worked are being compensated). Another interesting policy that increases the parents' flexibility is that parental leave does not have to be taken when the child is small. In contrast to most other countries, parents can split the leave into several shorter periods and can use it until the child turns eight. That way, parents could potentially use part of their parental leave to cover school holiday periods, taking time off work to supervise their child. This allows women not only to return to the labour market when the child is still young but enables them to work longer hours when the child gets older, as they can use up part of their parental leave days or hours when the child needs more attention. In fact, allowing parents to take off not only whole weeks, but to use their leave just for certain days or even hours provides mothers and fathers with a high degree of flexibility to care for their child when regular childcare facilities are closed, or when more attention is needed for their parental duties. The high flexibility that comes with parental leave allowances–both in regard to parents being able to share the leave according to their needs and to take the actual leave when most needed–has a considerable positive impact on fertility and female labour force participation in Sweden. Being able to use one's leave allowances when needed the most helps women to remain part of the labour force even when they have small children.

When discussing leave policies, it should not remain unmentioned that Swedish law also guarantees that both mothers and fathers can return to their previous employment after their official leave period. While the position could potentially be slightly different to the work before the leave (which rarely is the case), the law stipulates that the level of work has to be equal to the previous role. While a similar law, which guarantees that mothers and fathers can return to their previous employer after their childcare duties, also exists in Japan, the work does not have to be the same level. As a result, there is a hidden practice of assigning mothers (or fathers) who return to work and are no longer needed after their parental leave to lower positions with tedious work. The idea behind is that the boring work might lower their mood and satisfaction and discourage parents to keep working, with the result that they quit.

While maternity/paternity harassment (under which the previous practice falls) is relatively common in Japan–among pregnant working women alone, over 21% were harassed by their superiors and coworkers according to the Japan Institute for Labour Policy and Training (2016)–, this practice is nearly unheard of in Sweden, which is a sign that gender equality and the acceptance of working mothers with small children is more widespread in the Nordic country.

4) Social welfare policies: sick child leave, flexible work arrangements & options for part-time work

In order to combine family and employment, one needs a high degree of flexibility and support. Understanding that having small children sometimes does not allow the mother to be present at work every day, Swedish law states that parents can use part of their parental leave until the child turns eight, or the end of grade 1 of elementary school. If a child under 12 is sick, mothers or fathers can take paid sick childcare leave ("vård av barn" or VAB). If the child is sick child at home, unable to attend nursery or school, guardians can take up to 120 days per child p.a. off work. In addition to illness, accompanying the child to the doctor or dentist qualifies as a reason to take sick childcare leave. While parents do not receive full pay during these days, compensation is nearly 80% of their estimated income, up to an annual earning threshold of just under SEK 350,000 (€33,445) (Forsakringskassan, n.d.). Such support makes this family policy another important tool to help women remain part of the workforce even if they have young children.

Another factor contributing to mothers' high employment rate in Sweden are the flexible work arrangements many Swedish companies offer both voluntarily and because it is required by law. As discussed earlier, parental leave can be taken on hourly, daily or weekly basis, allowing parents to be with the child when their presence is most useful. Also, the chance to reduce working hours by up to 25% between the end of the parental leave and the child's eighth birthday helps parents to work flexibly (Nordic Council of Ministers, 2019b).

Although not stipulated by law, Swedish companies tend to be relatively flexible. According to data by Eurofound (2021), the European Foundation for the Improvement of Living and Working Conditions, about half of the companies with more than ten employees offer flexible working hours (flextime). Flexible working arrangements allow employees to set the start and end time of their day individually, within a given timeframe. In most cases, employees can start between 7:00 and 9:00 in the morning, take a lunch break (of at least 30 min) between 11:30 and 13.30, and leave work between 15:00 and 19:00. This flexible scheduling means that parents can adjust their workday to their child's schedule. In other words, due to flextime arrangements, many parents can drop off their children on the way to work and pick them up on the way back home, which reduces idle time and allows parents to use their time most efficiently. The European Company Survey 2019 suggests that as many as 80% of Swedish workess in half of the companies with ten or more employees have flexible working hours (Eurofound and Cedefop, 2020). Especially in larger companies, flexible work arrangements have been the norm, even before the Covid-19 pandemic. According to a global survey covering over 7,700 businesses in close to 40 countries, Sweden ranked second in terms of flexible work arrangements in 2010, with a whopping 86% of all surveyed companies offering flexibility in regard to working hours. In Japan, this was just the case in a mere 18% of all surveyed companies (Walter, 2011). The possibility of accumulating overtime and exchanging it for days off is widely practiced in most Swedish companies, with 73% of all employees being able to do so–20% more than the EU average. This allows workers to generate more paid holidays when needed, for example to care for their children when schools or nurseries are closed.

The chance to reduce working hours and to work part-time further helps mothers to combine childrearing duties and work. Yet, unlike in Japan, part-time only implies reduced working hours. In most cases, in Sweden, the content of the work, the hourly remuneration and the social security benefits offered to mothers working part-time is no different from their full-time position. In Sweden, around 30% of women work part-time. As only 21.6% of all female part-time workers in Sweden are in involuntary part-time arrangements, it can be concluded that most Swedish mothers have deliberately reduced their working hours to care for their children and that they are happy with their situation (Eurofound, 2021).

In Sweden, over 70% of all working women were employed in the public sector in 2015–the highest share in the EU (OECD, 2015). A major reason for the preference of the public sector (e.g. health, education, childcare, administrative work) among working mothers is the flexibility it offers regarding reduced working hours. As a result, a considerable share of women working for the Swedish government are on part-time contracts, with most of them having reduced their working hours after childbirth. Since the outbreak of the Covid-19 pandemic in 2020, remote work from home has become the new normal, with 32% of all survey participations working solely from home, and 21% from both the office and home in spring 2021. While this share is considerably lower than in spring 2020, 70% of all interviewees express a wish to also be able to work from home (in addition to the office) in the future (Netigate, 2021). This shows the changing nature of the workplace, which could potentially benefit women. Working from home not only means higher flexibility and the chance to have short breaks to care for their children (e.g. to pick them up) during the workday, it also reduces the time spent on commuting, allowing women to have a more productive time management. Thus, it can be concluded that the great flexibility of most Swedish work arrangements, especially for parents with children under eight, is another major factor for the country's high female labour force participation because it allows women to manage their time most efficiently, enabling them to continue employment while raising children.

5) Considerable male contributions to childcare and household chores

The last factor investigated here that contributes to the high labour force participation of Swedish mothers is a relatively high degree of gender equality in the household, with fathers being involved in household chores more than in all other European countries. With 56% of all Swedish men cooking or doing housework each day, their share is around 70% higher than the EU average, where just about one third (34%) of males perform household tasks on a daily basis (Statista, 2018). Sweden stands out as the country with the lowest difference between men and women's daily contributions to the household. While in Greece, for example, women are over five times more likely to do household chores on a daily basis than men (85% vs. 16%), Statista (2018) shows that the difference in Sweden is just a mere 18% (56% for men, 74% for women).

OECD data from 2015 reveal a similar trend, confirming the high degree of gender equality in Sweden. Assessing how much time people in OECD countries spend on unpaid work such as child and adult care, household chores, shopping, and volunteering, among others, Sweden ranks at the bottom of all 31 countries surveyed in terms of time spent by women on unpaid work, while also displaying the lowest gender gap in unpaid work, together with Denmark and Norway (OECD, 2018). At 3h 26min per day, Swedish women spend just under half as much time on unpaid work than females in Mexico, while Swedish men 'only' spend around 1 hour less on household chores and childcare than women per day. In Japan, the gender gap in unpaid work is the highest among all OECD countries, with Japanese men contributing less than 45 minutes of their time to unpaid work–a figure even lower than in neighbouring Korea. Japanese women, in contrast, spend 3h 44min per day engaged in unpaid activities–around five times more than men. Analysing the time spent on childcare and household chores among married couples in Japan, Statista (2021) comes to a similarly dismal result: while wives spent as much as 454 min (7h 34min) per day on household chores and childcare, husbands only contributed 83 min (1h 23min) of their time in 2016. Similar to the OECD research, the gender difference in Japan is a whopping 500%.

The data reveals that Sweden and Japan stand at the opposite ends of the spectrum when it comes to gender equality and the division of labour at home. While Swedish men's contributions in the household and in childcare allow a large share of women (with and without children) to engage in paid work, the low engagement of Japanese men with cleaning, cooking and looking after their children hinders many Japanese women from having a paid job or from increasing their working hours.

Conclusion

Sweden has a long history of family-friendly policies and a flexible labour market that supports universal employment. Since at least the 1970s, the Swedish Social Democrats have pushed for more gender equality by advancing the country's universalist welfare state regime. As a result, since the 1980s, women have reached a significant share of the labour force, and with more than 80% of Swedish women being gainfully employed in 2018, the gender gap in employment has become marginal (Eurostat, 2019). To the surprise of many, and in contrast to most other European countries, motherhood does not have a negative impact on women's labour force participation; indeed, there is a positive correlation between children and employment among both men and women. One reason for this is that, for decades, Sweden has propagated the dual-earner model and implemented policies that enabled men and women to share work, household chores and childcare equally. The comprehensive support for working parents, such as sick childcare leave, the possibility to reduce working hours by up to 25% until the child reaches third grade of primary school, and flexible working arrangements, in addition to generous maternity and parental leave benefits and universal state-supported childcare, allows Swedish women (and men) to combine parenthood and professional development. Sweden's high uptake of parental leave by fathers, who could potentially spend up to 390 days caring for their child, as well as sufficient childcare for children under one, enable women to return to work relatively soon after childbirth and reduces the likelihood that they remain outside the labour force for years.

This chapter has highlighted that the provision of universally available, high-quality childcare for kids under three is an important tool in Sweden's quest to promote high female employment. This, in addition to Sweden's flexible work arrangements, where employees themselves can set the start and end time of their workday within a given timeframe, and the option to reduce working hours while the child is young, helps Swedes to balance work and parenthood. Having fathers contribute to household chores and childcare, with the gender gap in unpaid work being the smallest in the EU and among OECD countries, means women in Sweden can engage in paid work to a similar degree as men.

It goes without saying that while the Swedish welfare state has achieved considerable gender equality and high female labour force participation, even Sweden is not 'perfect', and a gender gap regarding employment, the content of work, and remuneration exists. Swedish women's paid work averages around 149 hours a month–16h less than their male counterparts. In other words, men do not only have a slightly higher employment rate, but also work longer hours. Also, the pay per hour is higher for men than for women, averaging at €21.50 and €18.91, respectively. This wage difference is due to several factors: first, women tend to leave the workforce longer than men to care for children, which reduces their work experience; second, women often tend to choose lower paid professions (e.g. working in health, childcare, social work or administration) while more men graduate from STEM degrees and land higher paid jobs; third, women are overrepresented in the public sector (where wages are moderate) while men tend to work more in private companies, where salaries can be (re)negotiated on a regular basis, leading to a quicker rise in income. Fourth, many women tend to be less eager to demand higher salaries or a promotion, and often get offered lower salaries in negotiations than their male counterparts, even if they have the same skills and experience. Fifth, and last, women are underrepresented in middle- and senior management positions, and thus often miss out on larger salaries.

Yet, the gender pay gap is, according to OECD data, relatively small in Sweden: at 7.4%, it is only a third of that of Japan, where women on average earn 22.5% less than men for similar work (OECD, n.d.). The Swedish government suggests that the difference in women and men's unadjusted average salary was 9.8%, or a mere 4.4% when adjusted for the difference in profession and sector where men and women worked. Thus, while a gender wage gap also exists in Sweden, it is considerably lower than in other European countries, making it another example where Sweden leads the way in gender equality. With 40.2% of all managers and 38% of all board members of the largest publicly listed companies being female in 2019, Sweden is ahead of most other OECD countries, where the average is 33.2% and 26.7%, respectively (OECD, 2022b). The difference between Japan and Sweden is especially striking, with women holding less than 15% of all managerial roles in 2019 (OECD, 2022a).

While Japan ranks a dismal 120th out of 156 countries in the Global Gender Gap Report 2021 (and 147th in terms of political empowerment of women), Sweden has long been among the top performing countries in regard to gender equality. Ranked No. 5 in the Global Gender Gap Report 2021 and No. 1 in the EU's Gender Equality Index 2021, Sweden can be considered a role model in terms of gender equality (WEF, 2021). With policies that promote female political, economic, and social participation deeply entrenched in Swedish law and society, female labour force participation and the dual earner model among families have become a norm in Sweden.

Thus, it seems clear that it is the liberal social mindset, social norms that promote equality, generous family policies, and flexible labour market conditions that contribute to Sweden's high employment rate among women and mothers.

References:

Duvander, A.-Z. and Löfgren, N. (2019). Sweden country note. In Koslowski, A., Blum, S., Dobrotić, I., Macht, A., and Moss, P. (eds.) *International Review of Leave Policies and Research 2018*, 1–9. Retrieved from https://www.leavenetwork.org/fileadmin/user_upload/k_leavenetwork/annual_reviews/Leave_Review_2018.pdf

Eurofound and Cedefop (2020). *European Company Survey 2019: workplace practices unlocking employee potential. European Company Survey 2019 series.* Luxembourg: Publications Office of the EU

European Commission (2017). *European semester thematic factsheet: Women in the labour market.* Retrieved from https://ec.europa.eu/info/sites/default/files/european-semester_thematic-factsheet_labour-force-participation-women_en_0.pdf

European Commission (2018). *1 in 3 children in the EU now has access to high-quality and affordable childcare, Commission report shows.* Retrieved from https://ec.europa.eu/newsroom/just/items/625317

European Commission (2021). *Sweden: Early childhood and school education funding.* Retrieved from https://eacea.ec.europa.eu/national-policies/eurydice/content/early-childhood-and-school-education-funding-80_en

European Commission (n.d.). *Sweden: Parental benefits and benefits related to childbirth.* Retrieved from https://ec.europa.eu/social/main.jsp?catId=1130&intPageId=4808&langId=en

European Foundation for the Improvement of Living and Working Conditions (Eurofound) (2021). *Living and working in Sweden.* Retrieved from https://www.eurofound.europa.eu/ga/country/sweden

European Institute for Gender Equality (2021). *Gender Equality Index 2021.* Retrieved from https://eige.europa.eu/gender-equality-index/2021/country/SE

European Institute for Gender Equality (n.d.). *Sweden.* Retrieved from https://eige.europa.eu/countries/sweden

Eurostat (2019). *Employment rate of people aged 20 to 64 in the EU reached a new peak at 73.2% in 2018.* Retrieved from https://ec.europa.eu/eurostat/documents/2995521/9747515/3-25042019-AP-EN.pdf/b226fab2-566d-4dad-a830-a22b9fa5c251

Eurostat (2020). *Women's employment in the EU.* Retrieved from https://ec.europa.eu/eurostat/de/web/products-eurostat-news/-/EDN-20200306-1

Forsakringskassan (n.d.). *Employee with sick child (VAB).* Retrieved from https://www.forsakringskassan.se/english/parents/care-of-a-sick-child-vab

Gustafsson, S. and Jacobswson, R. (1985). Trends in Female Labor Force Participation in Sweden. *Journal of Labor Economics*, 3 (1), 256–274

Japan Institute for Labour Policy and Training (2016). *Ninshin-tō o riyū to suru furieki toriatsukai oyobi sekushuaruharasumento ni kansuru jittai chōsa: kekka* [Results of the fact-finding survey on disadvantageous treatment and sexual harassment due to pregnancy]. Press Release 1 March 2016. Retrieved from https://www.jil.go.jp/press/documents/20160301.pdf

Netigate (2021). *How do Swedish employees want working from home to be handled after the pandemic?* Retrieved from https://www.netigate.net/wp-content/uploads/2021/02/Working-from-home-after-the-pandemic.pdf

Nordic Council of Ministers (2006). *Nordic experiences with parental leave and its impact on equality between women and men.* Copenhagen: TemaNord. Retrieved from http://norden.diva-portal.org/smash/get/diva2:701827/FULLTEXT01.pdf

Nordic Council of Ministers (2019a). *Flexible work arrangements: the Nordic gender effect at work.* Retrieved from https://norden.diva-portal.org/smash/get/diva2:1240047/FULLTEXT02.pdf

Nordic Council of Ministers (2019b). *The Nordic Gender Effect at Work.* Retrieved from https://www.gu.se/sites/default/files/2020-05/The-nordic-gender-effect-at-work.pdf

OECD (2006). *Starting strong II: Early childhood education and care.* Paris: OECD Publishing. Retrieved from https://www.oecd.org/education/school/37423778.pdf

OECD (2015). *Government at a glance 2015: Country factsheet Sweden.* Retrieved from https://www.oecd.org/gov/Sweden.pdf

OECD (2017). *Japan policy brief: Employment.* Retrieved from https://www.oecd.org/japan/japan-improving-the-labour-market-outcomes-of-women.pdf

OECD (2018). *Balancing paid work, unpaid work and leisure.* Retrieved from https://www.oecd.org/gender/balancing-paid-work-unpaid-work-and-leisure.htm

OECD (2022a). *Employment: Female share of seats on boards of the largest publicly listed companies.* Retrieved from https://stats.oecd.org/index.aspx?queryid=54753

OECD (2022b). *Employment: Share of female managers.* Retrieved from https://stats.oecd.org/index.aspx?queryid=96330

OECD (2020). *OECD family database: LMF1.2: Maternal employment rates.* Retrieved from https://www.oecd.org/els/family/LMF1_2_Maternal_Employment.pdf

OECD (n.d.). *Key charts on employment.* Retrieved from https://www.oecd.org/gender/data/employment/

OECD (2022c). *LFS by sex and age–indicators.* Retrieved from https://stats.oecd.org/Index.aspx?DataSetCode=lfs_sexage_i_r

Statista (2018). *Who's doing European housework?* Retrieved from https://www.statista.com/chart/15880/housework-europe-gender-split/

Statista (2021). *Time spent on housework among married couples in Japan in 2016, by gender.* Retrieved from https://www.statista.com/statistics/858352/japan-time-spent-housework-by-gender/

Walter, L. (2011). Finland, Sweden, Australia offer most flexible work schedules. *EHS today.* Retrieved from https://www.ehstoday.com/archive/article/21904410/finland-sweden-australia-offer-most-flexible-work-schedules

World Bank (2021). *Labour force participation rate, female (% of female population ages 15–64) (modeled ILO estimate)–Sweden.* Retrieved from https://data.worldbank.org/indicator/SL.TLF.ACTI.FE.ZS?locations=SE

World Economic Forum (2021). *Global Gender gap report 2021*. Retrieved from https://www3.weforum.org/docs/WEF_GGGR_2021.pdf

II

Coming to work: why have so many (young) people from Poland and Romania moved to the UK?

Abstract   When in 2004, ten countries joined the European Union, the vast majority of old member states (EU-15) were afraid of overwhelming levels of labour mobility from East to West. Thus, in the Treaty of Accession 2003, a seven-year transition period was introduced, during which citizens of the new member states (namely Poland, Czech Republic, Hungary, Slovakia, Slovenia, Lithuania, Latvia, Estonia, Malta, and Cyprus) were granted the right of free, unrestricted movement of people only gradually. The UK was one of the few countries (with Ireland and Sweden) that did not make use of this right, allowing free movement of labour for all new member states from the date of their accession (May 1st, 2004). This liberal approach to immigration, coupled with the favorable condition of the British labour market in the mid-2000s, encouraged millions of citizens from the EU's eastern countries to move to the UK, entering the British labour market on an unprecedented scale.

Their impact on the British economy and society has been considerable, and migrants from the new member states (A-8 and A-2)[1] have contributed to funding the British social security system through their tax payments, increased productivity and innovation in some sectors of the economy, and relieved labour shortages, especially in hospitality, construction, agriculture, and the care sector. Yet, due to Brexit and the improving labour market in their

---

[1] A-8: the 10 accession countries that joined in 2004, minus Malta and Cyprus, two southern European islands; A-2: Romania and Bulgaria, the countries that joined in 2007.

home countries, the last few years have seen several hundred thousand eastern European workers leave the UK again.[2] While this has caused labour shortages in Britain, it also has the upside of 'brain circulation'–the possibility for countries with high outward migration to use the skills, know-how and experience of their migrants.

This chapter outlines the multiple, often interdependent reasons why over a million Poles and nearly half a million Romanians moved to the UK to work after their countries' accession to the EU, looking at economic, political, and social factors. It shows that while there was not a single main trigger, higher wages as well as better employment and career chances were predominant reasons for many of the Poles and Romanians moving to the UK. The lack of strong competition from other EU countries, who had a less liberal approach to immigration in 2004, helped make the UK into one of Europe's top two destinations for migrant workers from the new member states.

> While it took the EU over forty years to grow from its initial six member states to 15, the nine years between 2004 and 2013 saw the number of member states nearly double, to reach 28 in 2013.

> The uncertainty after the Brexit vote in 2016, outbreaks of xenophobia following it, and the ending of free movement with the UK's exit from the EU in January 2021, as well as the Covid-19 pandemic, caused around 300,000 Poles to leave British shores between 2017 and 2020. In 2021, the number of Polish-born residents in the UK fell below 700,000 people, marking a 33% decline since 2017.

---

[2] The new British immigration regime allows EU migrants living in Britain before 1 January 2021 to stay in Britain, but prospective new migrants from the EU require work permits which are subject to minimum income thresholds.

What this chapter covers: Migration, labour mobility in the EU, Poland, Romania, UK, labour market, social conditions in Romania, wages, migrant communities, push & pull factors for migration

> Unprecedented growth: The foreign-born population in the UK grew by over 80% in the 15 years 2004-2019, from 5.3 million in 2004 to almost 9.5 million in 2019. Despite Brexit, in 2021 around 3.6 million EU nationals still resided in the UK.

Introduction

While at the time of the EU's eastern enlargement in 2004, the number of Poles residing in the UK was, at under 70,000 people, marginal, within just ten years, they became the largest minority group in the UK In 2015, Poles outnumbered even the Indian-born population of the UK, reaching a peak of 1,021,000 people in 2017, though falling thereafter (ONS, 2015 & 2018). The UK not only became a favourite destination for young Polish workers, but also for many other eastern European nationals, hosting around 20% of all EU migrants since 2004 and currently being home to about 3.6 million EU-born citizens (Vargas-Silva/Walsh, 2020).[3] Yet, despite this general popularity, around a third of all migrants residing in the UK have come from just two countries: Poland and Romania. In 2019 these were the two biggest EU-born minorities in the UK, with in excess of 800,000 and 400,000 citizens respectively living in the UK. This leads us to the following question: What made Britain so attractive for citizens of these two countries?

This chapter outlines potential reasons behind the UK's rise to becoming the top destination for well over 1.5 million Poles and

---

[3] The European Commission puts the number of EU citizens in the UK at 2.6 million.

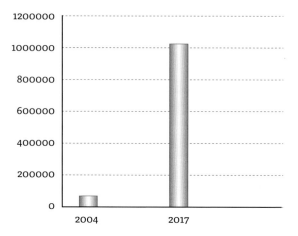

Fig. 2–1 Number Polish residents in the UK, 2004 and 2017

(ONS, 2015 & 2018)

Romanians.[4] We will look both at the **pull factors** that could have attracted them to the UK after their country's EU accession, and at the **push factors** that might have contributed to their decision to leave their country for the UK.

> **Push Factors:** negative factors in one's home country that make citizens want to leave
>
> **Pull Factors:** positive aspects attracting people to a different country (e.g., job vacancies, employment, and career opportunities)

Comparing the economic aspects of life in the UK and in Poland and Romania such as

· wages

---

[4] While in 2019, only around 1,250,000 citizens with Polish and Romanian nationality resided in the UK, it is estimated that well over 1.5 million citizens from these two countries have lived in the UK at some stage since 2004, with several hundred thousand having returned to their home country or moved somewhere else at some stage.

- the labour market and working conditions
- social and political factors such as an open, tolerant, and diverse society
- respect of the rule of law and press freedom
- the political system and good governance, among many others

this chapter shows that while economic reasons and career development have constantly been the number one motives for migration, factors such as efficient government, a high level of equality, generous social welfare and an open-minded society also played a significant role.

Definitions:

Migrant/immigrant: a person who goes to live and work in a country other than his/her own either temporarily or in order to settle there permanently. In the context of the EU, the terms migrant and immigrant often refer to non-EU citizens (so called third-country nationals, or TCNs).

Mobile EU citizen/mobile worker: Strictly speaking, in legal terms, an EU citizen residing in another EU country is not a migrant or immigrant, but a mobile citizen. This is because citizens of EU member states enjoy free, unrestricted mobility ("freedom of movement") to live, work or study in another member state under Article 21 of the Treaty on the Functioning of the EU (TFEU). Since 1992, there is no visa or special permission required for EU citizens to reside and work in another EU country, and no EU member state can restrict movement of other EU citizens to their country.

The EU's eastern enlargement in 2004, the implications for labour mobility, and the UK's liberal immigration policies in the mid-2000s

In 2004, as many as ten new countries with a combined population of nearly 75 million people joined the European Union, raising the number of member states from 15 to 25 overnight. This first round of eastern enlargement was not only special for its sheer size, but also because GDP, wages, and living conditions were significantly lower in the new member states. Due to this stark income gap, governments in most of the 15 'old' EU member states (commonly referred to as EU-15) feared that their countries could be 'overrun' with cheap labour from the new member states. As a result, all EU-15 countries but the UK, Ireland and Sweden made use of their right to restrict the freedom of movement for people from the new member states (A-10) during a seven-year transition people, and only gradually granted them the same freedom of movement citizens from the old member states have had since 1992.

Why did the UK take such a liberal stance on immigration in 2004, and what implications did it have for labour mobility to the UK? The main reason why Britain threw open its borders to migrants from the accession countries in 2004 was the ruling Labour Party's belief that the UK needed more immigration to support its economy, which was growing at a significantly higher pace than in the rest of the EU between 2004 and 2008 and had a considerably more buoyant labour market than the average EU-15 country. In 2004, employment in the UK was 5% above the EU average, while the unemployment rate was only just over half that of other EU-15 countries (4.7% and 8.2%, respectively) (Mlady, 2005). Given the rising demand for labour, Prime Minister Tony Blair was convinced that the UK could benefit from eastern European workers, most of whom were educated and well trained in their home country, and who would apply their skills and knowledge in UK businesses. Workers from the EU's eastern member states were especially welcome in certain sectors with rising labour shortages, such as social care, hospitals, agriculture, and hospitality. An additional reason why the UK government did not restrict movement from A-10 countries in 2004 was because it expected most of the other member states not to do so either and on that basis had considerably underestimated the number who would come (Watt/Wintour, 2015). All these reasons led to a relatively permissive, liberal immigration regime under the ruling Labour government.

It can be concluded that the tight labour market situation and growing labour shortages in several sectors were the main reason why the UK gave citizens from the EU's new member states unrestricted access to its market in 2004, although it should be noted that it was working on the assumption of much lower numbers arriving than turned out to be the case. But what were the reasons for millions of A-8 and A-2 country nationals to move to the UK after their country's accession? In the next section, we will look at the UK's pull factors that attracted new EU workers.

> **Poles abroad**
> According to a survey from 2013, about 14% of adult Poles worked abroad at some stage between 2004 and 2013, and as many as 69% had a family member or close friend living abroad. Poland's Central Statistical Office (2013) estimated that by 2007, just three years after EU accession, the Polish long-term diaspora abroad had reached 2.3 million.

Pull factors in the UK

Moving to a new country is always a big step. Thus, most migrants expect a payoff for the financial and emotional toll moving to foreign shores takes. Despite the wording, a payoff does not necessarily have to be financial, as not all migrants are motivated by a better standard of living. In fact, economic migration is just one type of migration.

Political scientists distinguish between four different migration patterns: 1) economic migration (to find work or to advance one's career); 2) social migration (to improve one's quality of life, to have more personal freedom and to be close to family, friends and partners); 3) political migration (to escape political persecution or war, or to leave a corrupt state or inefficient administration), and 4) environmental migration (to escape natural disasters or to live in a better natural environment). Teasing out the most common pull factors from within these four general types of migration in relation to the UK, we suggest that the most common pull factors–positive aspects of life in the UK–for Poles and Romanians moving to Britain after 2004 were the following:

- A better standard of living from higher wages
- A more buoyant labour market with low unemployment
- Good working conditions, such as higher labour standards, better equipment to work with, and sometimes a better work-life-balance
- Advanced social services and welfare, including healthcare, child benefits, pensions, and unemployment benefits
- A more tolerant, open society that allows people to fulfil their ambitions and live in accordance with their personal preferences
- Political stability and an efficient, trustworthy government practising good governance
- Strong respect for the rule of law and press freedom

While a clean environment as well as a good education system often also act as major pull factors, they probably only played a marginal role for mobility from Poland and Romania to the UK, and thus will be neglected in this chapter. Migration to the UK to pursue tertiary education will also not be included in this analysis as the numbers are negligible compared to those moving to the UK for the purpose of employment: statistics show that over 90% of migrants from A-8 and A-2 countries who moved to the UK between December 2005 and July 2006 did so for work purposes (and over 80% on average between 2004 and 2013) (Vargas-Silvas, 2014). Even from Poland, the largest new member state, only around 30,000 students attended British universities between 2004/05 and 2012/2013.

The UK is certainly not an ideal country; yet it ranks much higher on several of the above criteria than most eastern European countries, where social welfare, living standards, working conditions, salaries, good governance, and openness of society tend to be lower than in most western and northern European countries. In the following section, we will analyse to what extent the aforementioned pull factors (potentially) motivated Poles and Romanians to move to the UK to work, starting with economic pull factors (wages, employment and working conditions), followed by social conditions such as social welfare and the openness of society, and concluding with political factors such as efficient government, the rule of law, and press freedom.

1) Economic factors:

a) Wages in the UK

While not all Polish and Romanian migrants were motivated by the desire to improve their standard of living, economic migration best describes the majority of labour mobility from Poland and Romania to the UK. Especially in the early years after EU accession, a huge disparity in wages existed between the East and the West, and wages in the UK were often several times higher than in their home country. Although the wage gap is closing, salaries remain the main pull factor for most EU migrants. This is evident from a 2018 survey of 1,000 working-age Bulgarians residing in their home country but contemplating working abroad, which revealed that for a whopping 95% of them higher pay was a major pull factor. The desire for a higher standard of living was cited nearly twice as often as the second most common pull factor, better social systems (50%) (Kalfin/Kyuchukov, 2018).

The hope to better themselves financially motivated hundreds of thousands of Poles and Romanians to move to the UK after 2004. This can be best understood from the following figures on GDP and median wages in Poland, Romania, and the UK.

Annual per capita GDP (in US$) in 2004

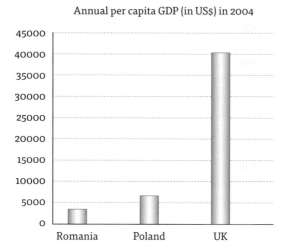

Fig. 2–2 Comparison of GDP in Romania, Poland, and the UK in 2004

(The World Bank, 2021a and 2021b)

GDP is the most common measure of a country's prosperity. In 2004, at the date of Poland's EU accession, annual GDP per capita stood at US$ 6,681 in Poland, whereas the UK's GDP passed the $40,000 mark in 2004 (and the $50,000 mark in 2007) (The World Bank, 2021a & 2021b). While this difference between Poland and the UK is already substantial, with the UK's GDP six time higher, the eleven-fold difference between the UK and Romania's GDP of $3,494 the same year is even more striking. Such enormous differences in GDP represented a massive national wealth gap between many western European countries like the UK and its eastern neighbours such as Poland and Romania, which still persists today, albeit at a lower level.

Another indicator of the financial well-being of a county and its people are wage levels. In 2004, the average monthly gross wage or salary in Poland was PLN 2,289 (around €500)–less than a quarter of the average in the UK, which was £1,834. Romania, in the year of its EU accession, had an average net wage or salary of around RON 1,042 (approx. €210) per month (Statista, 2021a). If we convert this into disposable income per family member per year (median equivalised net annual income), the figure for Romania, even in 2015, amounted to as little as €2,315 per annum–less than half of that in Poland (€5,560), and just around a tenth of the median equivalised disposable income per family member in the UK (€21,029) (Eurostat, 2022b). This shows how little chance the average worker in Romania, or in Poland for that matter, had of being able to save money unless they worked abroad. For a person on the minimum wage of PLN 824 (approx. €195) per month in Poland or RON 280 (approx. €60) per month in Romania in 2004, even making ends meet was a struggle (Statistics Poland, 2018).

But not only minimum wages were low: in Romania, even highly skilled people, like university professors or engineers, only earned an average salary of $600 per month in 2005. Professors received around $511–around twice the salary of dentists ($251)–, and engineers about $365 a month. It was reported in 2010 that "salaries for young doctors in Romania are 10 to 15 times lower than in Western Europe", with young resident doctors typically earning as little as €200 (Eurostat, 2021a).

As a result of the low salaries and often unsatisfactory working conditions in skilled, high-demand professions such as medicine, several thousand Romanian medical professionals moved to the UK, where even in 2004 average total earnings for nurses stood at £26,400 (around €31,600) (NHS, 2005). This means that although hundreds of Romanian doctors were working in the UK as nurses because their qualifications were not recognised, they were still earning several times what they would have earned back home as qualified doctors. While doctors' salaries were raised to around RON 3,900, or around €790, per month in 2007, the income gap between Romania/Poland and the UK in most professions is still significant enough for it to make economic sense for workers from these two eastern states to move to the UK.

According to the Romanian health minister, over 25,000 doctors left the country between 2009 and 2019. In the UK alone, around 10,000 Romanian health care professionals (doctors and nurses) were employed in 2018.

> Around 2004, people working on McDonald's cash desks in the UK were paid around 5.5 times more than their counterparts in Poland. Even adjusted for the lower living costs in Poland, the difference was substantial. In PPP (purchasing power parity) terms, based on the Big Mac price index, employees earning McDonald's UK wages could buy over twice as many burgers as in Poland, with their salary.

b) Labour market conditions

When Poland joined the EU in 2004, unemployment hovered at around 19%, a figure nearly four times higher than the UK's 4.7%. Unemployment was particularly high in the less developed, more rural eastern parts of Poland. For example, in 2004 there was a tenfold difference in the unemployment rate between Dorset/Somerset in the UK (at 2.4%) and the 24.9% unemployment in Poland's Dolnośląskie region (Mlady, 2005).

As well as unemployment being high, the number of job vacancies was low, with only around 220,000 open positions in the whole of Poland in 2004. This situation contrasted starkly with that of the UK, where 600,000 job vacancies existed in the same year (Okólski/Salt, 2014). In terms of numbers of unemployed per vacancy, the difference is even more telling: while in the UK there were around 2.5 unemployed persons per vacancy, in Poland the figure stood at 13.5 in 2004. Such differences in the openings on the labour market available between Poland and the UK were not only present in 2004 but persisted during the first few years after Poland's EU accession, albeit at a lower level.

From the migration perspective, the rate of youth unemployment is even more telling than the general unemployment rate because the average EU migrant tends to be young. According to the European Commission, in the early period of east-west EU labour migration (2004–2008), nearly half (48%) of all those migrating were aged 15 to 29–nearly three (!) times more than the average share of this age group in the EU population in 2020 (European Commission, 2014). In Poland, youth unemployment at the time of accession was approaching 40%, making the UK with its low general and youth unemployment rates a sought-after destination, especially in the first few years after 2004.

Why was youth unemployment so high in Poland at the time of accession, and what did it mean for young Poles? Obviously, the main reason for the high number of Polish youngsters not in employment was the high general unemployment rate and the saturation of the labour market. Two other major factors, however, also contributed to this situation: insufficient qualifications and experience and excessively high expectations in terms of salaries and working conditions among the younger generation. Lacking the necessary skills or work experience, but still demanding high starting salaries, many young Poles failed to find satisfactory employment at home, and therefore joined the mass exodus of youngsters after 2004.

In the UK, most post-accession migrants succeeded in finding a job even without previous work experience. Contrary to the common stereotypes of migrants being 'lazy' and scrounging off welfare benefits, the employment rate for EU mobile workers since 2005 has consistently been above that of UK natives. In fact, in 2021, the difference in the employment rate was a striking 7% points in favour of EU migrants (82.5% vs. 75.5%) (Statista, 2021). Similarly, also the unemployment rate of EU-born workers has consistently been lower than that of the UK-born population, until the onset of the pandemic in 2020 caused unemployment among migrants generally to rise (Fernandez-Reino/Rienzo, 2022). The higher employment and lower unemployment among EU workers stems from the fact that most EU-born citizens moved to the UK in order to work, and not to be economically inactive, e.g. as housewives or students. The high labour market participation rate among Poles and Romanians in the UK was assisted by the fact that they found it relatively easy to find a job in the UK, thanks to the hundreds (if not thousands) of job agencies in Poland and Romania facilitating the job-hunting process, and the fact that many British companies were eager to hire (cheaper) foreign workers because of the rising labour shortages in low- and medium-skilled occupations, especially in construction, hospitality and agriculture. Companies in these sectors were unable to fill vacancies with domestic workers alone, and many of the newly arrived workers were willing to do jobs the UK population was increasingly reluctant to take up (especially in the 3D–dangerous, dirty, and demanding–category). The thousands of EU workers happy to do any kind of job, no matter how physically demanding and how much below their qualifications, and often for pay at (or even below) the minimum wage, were a great asset for many British companies. Not only could the companies fill vacancies, but the wage differential that often existed between Polish/Romanian and UK workers meant that the companies could reduce their labour costs and spend more on investment. In addition, many EU-born workers were flexible and hard-working, with a strong motivation to succeed and make money, which increased productivity.

Employment opportunities were not only to be found among British companies, but also in the migrant communities themselves. The rising number of migrants from Poland and Romania increased the demand for products (such as food and drinks from home) and services (e.g. such as restaurants, travel agencies, recruitment companies, estate agents, language schools or lawyers targeted at Poles and Romanians.) In other words, the migrants themselves, via their increased aggregate demand for products and services, created new employment opportunities, which thousands of their number took advantage of by setting up small businesses. Vargas-Silva/ Walsh (2020) reveal that as many as 22% of Romanian and Bulgarian migrants aged 16-64 were self-employed, offering their services to both the migrant and local communities.

At the time of the EU's eastern enlargement, unemployment was much higher in most new member states than in the UK, but since then things have changed dramatically. The fast economic growth in A-8 and A-2 countries after their EU accession and the huge exodus of their workers to other EU member states greatly reduced unemployment and gave rise to severe labour shortages in some countries and occupations. Eastern European member states now have among the lowest unemployment rates in the EU, with only two of the A-8 and A-2 countries above the EU average of 6.5% as of November 2021 (Statistisches Bundesamt, 2022). The Czech Republic, for example, with 2.2% unemployment in November 2021, has had the lowest unemployment rate in the EU for some years, and even Poland had an unemployment rate below Germany's in 2021 (3.2% vs. 3.0%) (Eurostat, 2022a). Thus, it can be concluded that a more buoyant labour market and better chances of finding employment in the UK than at home ceased to be important pull factors in recent years.

A good indication that the main motive of Poles who moved to EU-15 countries between 2004–2008 was economic, namely the search for employment, is the fact that in that period only 27% of Polish migrants had tertiary-level education, while in the period 2009–2013 the proportion was 41%. This suggests that in the first few years after Polish accession, purely economic reasons, and above all the unemployment at home, were the main reasons for going abroad, while for later migrants factors like advancing one's career, better social welfare and 'soft factors' like a more liberal society played a bigger role in their decision to move to other EU member states.

c) Career prospects

The lack of career prospects for new graduates and limited career opportunities among highly skilled young people already working were another (economic) pull factor that influenced the decision of young Poles and Romanians to move to the UK in search of a better career and higher job satisfaction. Despite many of them being considerably better educated than their older co-workers, they tended to receive much lower salaries and often had little chance of promotion to management positions because these were occupied by the older generation. Around the time of accession young Poles, even university graduates, were facing a very slack labour market, for two reasons. First, job creation was slow during the years in which the Polish post-communist economy was being restructured into a capitalist system. Secondly, the late 1970s and early 80s had seen a rise in fertility. The six years between 1979 and 1984 can be described as baby boom years, with 322,000 more births than in the preceding six years, and as many as 573,000 more babies than in the following six years (Okólski/Salt, 2014). With the average university graduate entering the labour market at age 23, this meant that the period 2002–2007–when these baby boomers were ready to enter the Polish labour market–coincided with the beginnings of their fee, no fee labour mobility within the EU. The baby boomers placed further strain on an already saturated domestic labour market, which could not absorb all of them. As many of the people trying to find employment in the early 2000s were more educated than their parents' and grandparents' generations and tended to have a better command of foreign languages, their aspirations were also higher than that of the average worker (Okólski/Salt, 2014). However, many Polish companies were not yet internationally oriented and were unwilling to pay the higher wages that many of the young graduates sought in return for their skills. The result was that tens of thousands of young Polish graduates left for the UK between 2004 and 2007 alone. In 2007, 29% of Poles relocating to the UK had not had a job prior to moving. While not all of these were fresh out of university–many also had only completed secondary schooling or had been unemployed in Poland before leaving for abroad–it can be assumed that the majority of those who secured their first employment in the UK were enterprising young graduates (Jaźwińska, 2013).

The workers who moved from Poland to the UK had a quite different outlook from those who went to work in Germany. Migrants to the UK were considerably more educated than their counterparts that relocated to Germany, which suggests that many young Poles chose the UK to advance their career or to find employment that would allow them to gain new skills. Even though many eastern European workers actually ended up working in jobs not matching their qualifications (about half of the skilled workers from A-8 countries were in low or medium-low skilled jobs in 2020 job satisfaction tended to be high (Fernandez-Reino/Rienzo, 2022). This was because their wages were well above what they would have earned back home and because many jobs still allowed for professional and personal development, including improving English language proficiency.

d) Working conditions

In 2018, Romania substantially increased doctors' salaries in an effort to stop its high-skilled medical professionals from leaving the country and to encourage health workers in the diaspora to return. However, few of the tens of thousands of Romanian doctors working abroad have done so. The Romanian health minister explained that the reasons were not just salaries but also working conditions (Romania Insider, 2019):

> As you can clearly see, the simple increase of salaries was not the solution to bring our doctors back, and so we have to work, first and foremost, on working conditions in hospitals. We need to raise our infrastructure to a European level, especially for our patients.

Satisfactory working conditions play an increasingly important role not only among UK nationals (especially the younger generation, who are often willing to trade a lower salary for a better work-life-balance and a more fulfilling job), but also for EU workers. While the UK was never among the top EU countries for work-life-balance, working conditions in the UK are often above-average in regard to how employees are treated, paid holiday entitlement, and workplace equipment and training. While millions of workers in the UK face overwork, stress, and a poor work-life balance, working conditions in Poland are often no better. As Eurofound (2021) notes, "work–life balance related problems are relatively more frequent in Poland than on average in the EU." In 2016, 63% of Polish respondents reported being too tired from work to do the household chores at few times a month, revealing also high levels of stress and physical exhaustion.

A factor contributing to low job satisfaction in Romania among many of its doctors was the lack of proper equipment in many hospitals, making it difficult for young doctors to practice what they have studied over several years at university. A lack of modern technical devices in many hospitals, poor hospital management and the general underfunding of the healthcare system in Romania has contributed to thousands of young Romanian doctors moving to EU countries with more modern hospitals. A doctor describes it with the following words: "Most hospitals in the country are in debt and even large university hospitals often lack basic supplies, such as surgical gloves and antibiotics [...]. I want to have the resources to practice real medicine, without worrying that basic drugs are not available in the hospital pharmacy or the CT scan is broken" (Haivas, 2010).

While the high salaries that countries like the UK offered young doctors were certainly the main pull factor, the closer analysis here shows that working conditions such as hospital equipment and management also contributed to the high labour mobility of medical professionals. For other workers, too, better equipment, management and a relatively good work-life-balance increased the attractiveness of British companies.

2) Social factors

a) Social security

Social welfare and the availability of support in times of need have a great impact on the mental and physical well-being of people. The absence of a comprehensive social welfare system, and the fear of being without the necessary support when in need, can be a considerable source of stress for many people. In addition, low social welfare spending can result in children growing up in poverty and at risk of social exclusion, which was still the case for nearly 40% of children in Romania in 2018 (Eurostat, 2020).

While the UK is not a classical welfare state and has a much less tight security net than for example the Nordic countries, social welfare provision and GDP spending on welfare have been considerably higher than in most A-8 and A-2 countries. Despite a recent increase in welfare spending in many of the EU's eastern member states, they still lag behind most of their western European peers, including the UK. In fact, all 13 new member states belong to the 15 countries with the lowest social welfare spending in relation to GDP in the EU (the other two being Luxembourg and Ireland, which have very high GDP and therefore a lower welfare spending relative to GDP) (Eurostat, 2021c).

At 15% of GDP, social expenditure in Romania was scarcely higher than half the EU average (26.9%), and with a GDP much lower than other EU countries, Romanian welfare spending in absolute figures was even further removed from the European average and that of the UK. In the UK, net social spending amounted to 23.3% of GDP in 2017, which both in relative and absolute terms was considerably higher than in countries like Romania or Poland.

Looking at how social welfare benefits are spent in Romania, it is striking that the bulk of state welfare expenditure goes to the elderly, to finance old-age pensions. Little spending is allocated to the millions of young Romanian workers, because expenditure on family policies, education and poverty relief, which benefit them most, is low. As "Romania directs a significantly lower share to benefits aimed at tackling social exclusion, unemployment and providing housing benefits" than the EU average, many young Romanians have received little support from the government (Adăscăliței et al., 2020). This, combined with the often poor targeting of social welfare benefits, low starting wages and the regressive redistribution of income and wealth means that life is a struggle for many Romanians. Take unemployment benefits: in Romania they are simply too low to live on. For new graduates without work experience, unemployment benefits are as little as RON 250 (around €50) a month, and even with at least a year of work experience, it is only RON 375 (around €75) (European Commission, n.d.). Although benefits increase with age and years in employment, they are considerably lower than the EU average and often not enough to protect those without work from poverty and social exclusion. In the aftermath of the recession of the early 2010s, the net replacement rate of unemployment benefits in Romania dropped sharply. By 2018 it was only around 32%, i.e., less than a third of the worker's previous salary (OECD, 2021). While unemployment benefits in the UK are also lower than in most other western European countries, the replacement rate at just above half (56%) of the previous salary in 2020 is still much higher than in Romania in relative and absolute terms (Adăscăliței et al, 2020).

An indicator of the low priority of alleviating poverty or supporting the weaker sections of society in Romania is the low share of social housing. 95% of the country's housing stock is in private hands and only 5% government-owned. Since barely a third of all government-owned housing is reserved for the socially disadvantaged, state subsidised housing (including social housing) amounts to a mere 1.5% of all housing (Adăscăliței et al, 2020).

Healthcare and education are two further sectors that are significantly underfunded in Romania. In 2019, only 5.7% of GDP–a meagre €661 per person–was spent on health care. This was only about half of what the British government spent on healthcare as a share of GDP (10.2% in 2019) and less than an eighth of what the Swedish government provides for healthcare in absolute figures (€5,042 Euro per person, p.a.) (ONS, 2021a). The result of Romania's vastly underfunded medical system is a lack of hospital beds and equipment, leading to relatively high infant mortality, long surgery waiting times, and a comparatively short life expectancy. In 2010, the sad state of the Romanian healthcare system and its hospitals was described by Haivas (2010) in the following terms:

> Most hospitals in the country are in debt and even large university hospitals often lack basic supplies, such as surgical gloves and antibiotics, forcing patients to pay for such amenities out of [their own] pocket. Many buildings are in serious need of repair and sanitization.

The Euro Health Care Consumer Index 2018 ranked Romania a dismal 34th out of 35 European countries, much below not only all other EU member states, but also worse than all non-EU European countries except Albania. After evaluating factors such as patient rights and information, accessibility (waiting times for treatment), health outcomes, range and reach of service, prevention, and pharmaceuticals, the Health Care Consumer Index concluded that "Romania does have severe problems with the management of its entire public sector". It is "suffering from an antiquated healthcare structure, with a high and costly ratio of in-patient care over out-patient care" and inefficient allocation of funds in healthcare (Health Consumer Powerhouse, 2019).

With the exodus of thousands of medical doctors after 2007–the Romanian College of Physicians reported in 2010 that more than 4,000 (mainly young) doctors had emigrated within the first three years of the county's EU membership–the dismal state of the

Romanian healthcare system was not only continuing but getting worse. The brain drain of medical professionals means that Romania nowadays has one of the lowest ratios of physicians to population in the EU (European Commission, 2021b). Several sources suggest that as many as half of Romanian doctors may have left the country between 2009 and 2015, and that about 10% of those remaining are actively recruited by headhunters to lure them to move to western EU member states (Armand, 2020). This brain drain, coupled with the greying of Romania's population, has led to a shortage of 40,000 qualified doctors. To ease the pressure on remaining doctors, many healthcare employees continue to practice after retirement. The average family doctor in Romania is over 50, and hundreds (if not thousands) of doctors practice beyond 65. While this has some advantages, having an elderly doctor or surgeon can put patients in serious danger, as mistakes and wrong medical decisions increase with old age.

That low healthcare funding and the shortage of doctors has negative impacts on the Romanian population can be seen from the high infant mortality in Romania, which at 5.8 deaths per 1,000 live births in 2019 was the second highest in the EU and over three times that of the best-performing country, Estonia (European Commission, 2021a). The American-based NPO Borgen Project (2020) describes the risk Romania's medical system can pose to its citizens in the following strong words: [Romania] consistently fails to provide quality care. Worse than being inadequate, Romanian hospitals are often dangerous. Poorly trained staff often do not follow proper medical procedures and expose patients to unsanitary conditions. They cite as an example a case from 2018 where an antibiotic-resistant superbug infected 39 babies in a maternity ward due to a lack of hygiene and proper medical practice.

Another indicator of insufficient healthcare is the comparatively low life expectancy at birth in Romania, which stood at 74.2 years in 2020. This was, after Bulgaria, the second lowest in the EU (Eurostat, 2021). In England, male babies born between 2018 and 2020 could expect to live over five years longer than Romanian babies (79.3 years); for baby girls, the life expectancy was nearly nine years longer than that of Romanian newborns (ONS, 2021b).

This stark difference reveals the huge gap in the standard of medical care and living conditions in the UK and Romania and suggests that the relatively good healthcare system in the UK potentially also functioned as a pull factor for Romanians emigrating to England.

Polish women residing in the UK have a higher fertility rate than those living in Poland, indicating that better living conditions, higher social welfare and a more sophisticated healthcare system can have a positive impact on fertility.

In 2018 and 2019 more babies were born to Romanian mothers abroad than in the country itself. This reveals the extent of emigration of young Romanians.

b) Gender equality and a tolerant society

While financial reasons have been a major motivation for the majority of young Poles and Romanians leaving for western European countries, non-monetary considerations have played an increasingly important role among recent EU migrants. These may include gender equality and sexual liberation, abortion rights, less entrenched gender norms, and liberal values. In the following, we will analyse how Romania and Poland compare to the UK in these respects.

The Gender Equality Index reveals a striking difference between the UK and both Poland and Romania. While the UK, with 72.7 out of 100 points, ranked fifth among EU countries in 2020, Poland and Romania received low scores and were only in 24th (55.8 points) and 26th (54.4 points) position, respectively (EIGE, 2020a & 2020b). In other words, Romania ranked not only over 20 places below the UK, but both Poland and Romania were among the least gender equal in the EU.

One of the biggest obstacles to gender equality in Poland lies in the powerful presence of the Catholic Church, whose social and political influence has grown in the post-Communist era. The Polish

Church has often pushed a conservative social agenda, limiting women's reproductive rights and helping enforce traditional gender roles in Polish society. As a result, Poland recently implemented a near-total ban on abortion (with the exception of pregnancies resulting from rape or putting women's life or health at risk), which make it one of the strictest in Europe. Gender norms (and thus certain expectations of how women should behave) remain deeply entrenched in Polish society, and despite the fact that under the Communist regime both spouses tended to work, contemporary Polish society still expects women to do most of the household chores and child-rearing tasks. As a result, Polish women tend to spend nearly 2.5 hours per day more on unpaid work than men, and 30 minutes more than the OECD average (OECD, n.d.b). Also, parental leave is predominantly only taken by women in Poland, with less than 3% of fathers taking time off work to care for their children (OECD, n.d.a).

Cultural norms and expectations also contribute to gender inequality in Romania, where women spend considerably more time on household chores and childcare, too. While this is the trend in all modern societies, partly because women on average do fewer hours of paid work than men, Romanian women's share of total unpaid work amounts to 67.9%, which is not only much higher than in northern and central Europe, but also the highest among all eastern European countries assessed by the International Labour Office (Charmes, 2019). Women in Romania spend an average of 264 minutes a day on unpaid domestic work, while for men it is only 125 minutes.

A further feature of a tolerant, liberal society is respect for LGBT rights. As both Romania and Poland are conservative and very religious, LGBT communities there have struggled to achieve social representation and equal rights. Unlike in the UK, same sex marriages are not allowed, and in Poland homosexual couples cannot adopt children. In recent years, LGBT rights have been pushed even further back in Poland: in 2021, several Polish regions planned to declare themselves LGBT-free zones. The proposals were only withdrawn when the EU threatened to freeze funding to these regions.

In contrast, LGBT rights in the UK have been improving steadily, and same-sex couples and marriages have become generally accepted. Thus, the lower incidence of discrimination based on sexual orientation may also have acted as a pull factor for migration to the UK.

3) Political factors

a) Corruption

While the majority of migrants from Romania and Poland certainly cannot be classified as political dissidents, dissatisfaction with inefficient government, infringement of the rule of law, a high level of corruption and lack of de-facto media freedom have also played a significant role in young Romanians' and Poles' decision to work in the UK. Analysing the differences in corruption, judicial independence and press freedom between Poland/Romania and the UK. it will be shown that in all these areas the UK fares much better than Romania or Poland.

According to Transparency International's Corruption Perceptions Index (CPI) 2021, Romania has the highest perceived levels of public sector corruption in Europe. On a scale of 0 (highly corrupt) to 100 (not corrupt), Romania scores 44, with Poland scoring 56, both considerably worse than the UK's 77 (Transparency International, 2021). In fact, the main reason for Romania not being allowed into the EU in 2004 were its weak systems and poor performance in fighting corruption. It was admitted in 2007 on condition that the rule of law was strengthened, anti-corruption efforts stepped up, and judicial independence guaranteed. Although the EU closely assesses the country's progress each year through the Cooperation and Verification Mechanism (CVM), not all reports are favourable. In October 2018, the Council of Europe also voiced its concerns about amendments to Romania's criminal code in a 26-page opinion paper, pointing out that the changes would affect the separation of powers and impede the fight against corruption (Council of Europe, 2018). In 2019, Romania was threatened with EU sanctions on the ground that "[r]ecent amendments to the criminal code risk creating a situation of de facto impunity for crimes, including corruption crimes," as Vice-President Frans Timmermans of the EU Commission wrote in a letter to Romania on May 10th, 2019.

A study of corruption by the European Greens revealed that as much as 15.6% of Romania's GDP is lost to corruption, a figure close to nine times what the government spent on education and five times its healthcare expenditure (The Greens/EFA, 2018). Surveys show how common corruption is in everyday life in Romania: for example, in one survey 25% of respondents reported having been asked for bribes when accessing public services, and more than two thirds said their daily lives were affected by corruption–the highest level in the EU. What is more, nearly half of all Romanians (46%) perceived corruption to be increasing, making them lose confidence in the political system at home, and potentially prompting a decision to move abroad.

b) Rule of law and press freedom

A recent deterioration of the rule of law and restrictions on press freedom in Romania and Poland may also have acted as a push factor for their citizens to relocate to the UK in the final years before Brexit. In 2019, the European Commission (2019: 3) issued the following statement of concern regarding the erosion of the rule of law in Romania:

> [M]ajor legislative changes, also outside the justice domain, [were] rushed through using urgency procedures with minimal consultation, [and] have damaged both the quality of legislation and public confidence in policymaking. Judges and prosecutors have continued to face misleading coverage and unduly personal attacks in the media, with mechanisms for redress falling short, ultimately affecting the reputation and the credibility of the justice system as a whole. Different branches of the State have again been in conflict, and increasingly these divisions are played out in the Constitutional Court, further increasing tensions and showing that loyal cooperation falls short.

Poland, too, has seen a severe restriction or erosion of judicial independence and press freedom in recent years under the ruling

Law and Justice Party (PiS) and President Andrzej Duda. Since coming to power in 2015, the government has gradually brought the appointment, promotion and disciplining of judges and prosecutors under its control. Political control undermines the independence of the judiciary, a basic principle of the rule of law, and Poland has become the first EU member state to place its courts under such control. In 2018 the European Court of Justice (ECJ) ordered Poland to repeal the offending legislation. The victory was short-lived, however, and far from giving up its attempts to control the judiciary, the government passed new legislation in 2018, allowing the Minister of Justice (and Prosecutor General) Zbigniew Ziobro to control the appointment of those responsible for all stages of the investigation, prosecution and adjudication of disciplinary proceedings against ordinary court judges. Ziobro "appointed new national disciplinary officials who began to initiate disciplinary investigations against judges openly critical of his efforts to subdue Poland's independent judiciary", according to the verdict of the European Stability Institute (European Stability Initiative, 2021). As this again meant that the judicial system was largely controlled by the government, the European Commission (2019) started further infringement proceedings against Poland in April 2019, on the ground that "the new disciplinary regime undermines the judicial independence of Polish judges by not offering necessary guarantees to protect them from political control, as required by the Court of Justice of the European Union."

Not only the courts, but also the Polish media have been losing independence, as the government has continued to restrict independent newspaper and broadcasting outlets. According to Reporters Without Borders (2021a), the Polish government has consolidated its control of state media by a campaign of 'repolonising' privately-owned media outlets through censorship. Part of this 'repolonisation' campaign was the acquisition of 20 of the 24 regional newspapers (with 17 million online readers) from the German-owned Polska Press by the state-controlled oil company Orlen. That rising state ownership or influence of the media can impact election results is not only apparent from Russia, Turkey, and Hungary, but was also seen in the 2020 elections in Poland, where President Duda's rivals were subjected to relentless attacks and attempts to discredit them by state-controlled newspapers and TV channels. Reporters Without Borders (2021b) considered the erosion of press freedom so serious as to declare a "press freedom state of emergency" in Poland in 2021, condemning the "arbitrary restrictions on press freedom that the government has imposed".

It can be concluded that the recent deterioration in the rule of law in both Poland and Romania, the attacks on press freedom and media impartiality in Poland, and rising levels of perceived corruption in Romania may have contributed to rising dissatisfaction particularly among the young and educated population. As a result, the comparatively strong rule of law, freedom of expression and media plurality in the UK, together with a relatively low (perceived) level of corruption, may have acted as further push factors for EU labour mobility from Poland and Romania to the UK.

What factors are most important?

Investigating possible economic, political, and social motivations for moving from Poland and Romania to the UK throws up a host of good reasons for labour mobility. What all these motivations have in common is the search for a better life, whether in terms of higher living standards, greater personal fulfillment, more individual freedom, or new chances for personal and professional development. It is hard to say which factors exactly weighed heaviest, not only because of the considerable variation in circumstances between different migrants, but because there is usually more than one motivation or expectation at work in any given case. The reasons for relocation are complex and multi-layered, and sometimes even for the migrants themselves it is hard to pinpoint which motivations were strongest.

It is safe to say, however, that what many people were seeking through migration was the higher satisfaction of their wants that taking advantage of the many new opportunities life in the UK (but not their home country) offered. When Britain's borders were thrown open to all A-8 citizens in 2004, a multitude of new opportunities opened up especially for young Poles, who were facing a youth unemployment rate of around 40% and low wages. Different studies have shown that the vast majority of Poles and Romanians emigrating to the UK did so predominantly for economic reasons, hoping for better wages, higher job satisfaction and more fulfilling careers. The lack of opportunities for young people, especially women, in Poland and Romania in the early years after their country's accession was thus a major push factor. Other significant reasons besides unemployment or underemployment, low productivity and lack of career chances included inefficient government, corruption, inequality, suffocating traditions and social norms, and a general lack of good governance in their home country. While the economic and social situation in their home countries has been improving over the years, especially in regard to wages and unemployment rates, the 'stick factors' that might discourage emigration (such as family, friends, traditional foods and social life) still often remain less powerful than the pull factors described above, especially for the EU's poorest countries. Thus, until Brexit ended free movement to the UK for EU citizens, labour mobility from the A-2 countries (Romania and Bulgaria) to the UK kept growing until the Covid-19 pandemic started. Even for Poland, the migration stream only began to decline in 2018.

Despite attempting an in-depth analysis of potential factors, we cannot claim that the results are conclusive. In addition to the economic, political, and social factors discussed in this chapter, other, more subtle considerations might have influenced people's decision to move. One could be pop culture: the TV drama series *The Londoners*, which appeared on Polish public TV in 2008, had over three million viewers, who came to see London as a vibrant and colourful city where everyone (despite many hardships) could succeed in life – and have fun at the same time. The prominent media presence of Britain and the positive portrayal of life in London might have been one of the things that triggered an interest in working in the UK.

Other factors not discussed in this chapter were language, a society welcoming to foreigners, the existence of established Polish and Romanian communities in the country, good transportation links from Poland, efficient job agencies that supported the move to the UK, and Britain's multicultural society. Most humans want to feel at home and part of a larger group. Thus, people tend to emigrate to places where there is already a community of people with the same ethnic background. These communities not only provide a support network and assistance in all kinds of areas (including finding a job), but also support the emotional well-being of the expatriates. Thus, the existence of Polish and Romanian communities from the very beginning, Polish shops, frequent flights and bus connections home, as well as professional help with job-hunting from agencies were probably other important reasons why so many Poles and Romanians chose London and the UK over other EU countries. The fact that the local language was English, a *lingua franca* (common language) throughout much of eastern Europe, was without doubt another powerful reason why Britain was such a popular destination, as knowledge of the local language facilitates integration into the community and makes everyday life easier.

Despite all this, the chapter shows that while the reasons for people's decision to move to the UK were complex and multi-faceted, the strongest pull-factors were economic, with most people moving to the UK for relatively well-paid employment. The fact that the UK opened its borders to accession country migrants well before most other EU member states gave it an important first-mover advantage and led to many Poles and Romanians choosing the UK over other countries. In addition, rising labour shortages in Britain at a time when, for example, in Poland, its mostly well-educated and English-speaking young people faced a 40% youth unemployment rate and lack of career opportunities, catapulted the UK into the number one spot as the most popular destination for EU mobiles.

Conclusion

The UK is the second most popular country, after Germany, for EU migration from eastern Europe, especially Poland and Romania. In 2017 there were 3.8 million EU nationals living in the UK–an increase of nearly 350% in 13 years, up from under 1.1 million in 2004

(Vargas-Silva/Walsh, 2020). The reasons for this unprecedented flow of EU migrants to the UK after the EU's eastern enlargement in 2004 are manifold, but centre around economic and social factors. Studies of mobile Polish workers' motivation for moving to the UK "consistently found that financial reasons, lack of opportunities in Poland and the desire for personal and professional development were key factors in decisions to migrate" (Okólski/Salt, 2013).

This chapter analysed the impact different economic, social, and political factors had on mobility from Poland and Romania to the UK. It shows that economic pull factors, such as high wages, a buoyant labour market with low unemployment, good career opportunities and decent working conditions played a major role in attracting foreign labour. Among social factors, we have seen several things that young Polish and Romanian workers would find attractive, such as the existence of a social security net, the openness of British society and the acceptance of people with different ethnic backgrounds and sexual orientation, including the LGBT community, and a high level of gender equality. A comparison of the political situation in Romania and Poland with that in the UK also pointed to the conclusion that guarantees of law and order, a clear separation of powers in the administration, press freedom and relatively efficient, uncorrupt government could also have played a role (at least in recent years) in attracting Polish and Romanian citizens disillusioned with the political situation in their home country to the UK.

There is no doubt that the high salaries in the UK, especially in the first few years after 2004 when Poles and Romanians would be able to earn as much in two or three months as they could in a year back home, acted as the main pull factor for most migrants from these countries. Push factors such as unemployment or underemployment at home, low productivity, lack of career chances, inefficient government, corruption and nepotism, social inequality, suffocating traditions and social norms, and a lack of good governance in their home countries further increased the desire of many eastern European nationals to move to the more prosperous, more socially advanced UK.

While an analysis on these lines has great explanatory power, it should not be forgotten that the rationale behind individual decisions to move to the UK to work is often complex and involves an interplay of many interdependent factors. In the end, most people who have emigrated did so because they saw chances they did not have at home–whether these chances were a higher salary, life in a more diverse and multicultural environment, or freedom from restrictive cultural norms at home. The UK became one of the most sought-after destinations for migrant workers from Poland and Romania because they offered these chances before most other EU countries, which only gradually granted citizens of the new member states full freedom of movement.

It can be concluded that there was no predominant single factor, but a host of significant economic, political, and social reasons why 1.5 million Poles and Romanians moved to the UK after 2004. This finding is not peculiar to the case of Polish and Romanian migrants to the UK, but applies to most post-accession migration from eastern Europe to EU-15 countries. Numerous empirical studies have found complex and diverse underlying causes of east-west migration. While an analysis of the pull and push factors is important for understanding the possible reasons for mass movements of population, and to gain an idea of what might have contributed to the decisions of many millions of individuals to leave their home to work in other EU member states, it cannot provide an exhaustive explanation of all the often strikingly different patterns and motivations for labour mobility in the EU.

It is also important to note that over time several of the pull factors attracting mobile Europeans to the UK have lost some of their power. The main reason has been the rapid economic growth in the new member states. Poland's unemployment rate fell below Britain's in 2018, wages have increased, and labour shortages and economic restructuring have improved career prospects for millions of eastern European workers. With new opportunities, improving living standards and greater satisfaction among the population of the home country, the attraction of emigration has decreased. Brexit has further weakened the pull to the UK and around 325,000 Poles have left Britain since 2016, the year of the Brexit referendum

(Statista, 2022b). This was certainly partly due to the more favourable economic situation in Poland. However, other factors behind this exodus were Brexit-related: increasing xenophobic sentiment among the domestic British population causing migrants sometimes to feel unwelcome, uncertainty about the rights of EU workers wishing to remain in the UK after Brexit, and the imminent ending of preferential free movement from the EU to be replaced by a system of work permits which would in future apply to all would-be immigrants, including those from the EU. In the case of the A-2 countries, the UK remained attractive longer–wages in Romania still remain much below the UK–and migration from both countries continued increasing until 2019, well after the EU referendum, though it fell in 2020, the last year of free movement, due to the Covid-19 situation.

The large number of Poles that have left the UK in recent years shows how temporary and fluid EU labour mobility is. Unlike immigration to the UK from outside the EU in the 20th century, which has mostly been long-term or permanent, EU labour mobility is often temporary, with workers returning to their home country or moving to another EU member state after gaining professional and personal experience in the host country. The main reasons for this often temporary nature of EU migration are not only modern telecommunication and cheap air travel, which have made it easy to keep close contact with family, friends and job agencies back home, but also because the economic, political and social conditions in the country of origin and the country of destination (pull and push factors) often change rapidly, affecting the tradeoffs between migration and remaining at home.

Thus, it can be concluded that while the push and pull factors certainly fail to provide one single answer as to why well over 1.5 million Poles and Romanians moved to the UK after 2004, they are a powerful tool in understanding some of the many reasons for post-accession labour mobility.

References

Adăscăliţei, D., Raţ, C. and Spătari, M. (2020). *Improving Social Protection in Romania.* Bucharest: Friedrich Ebert Foundation. Retrieved from http://library.fes.de/pdf-files/bueros/bukarest/16834.pdf

Armand, C. (2020). Eastern Europe gives more to the west than it gets back. *Financial Times.* 14 February 2020. Retrieved from https://www.ft.com/content/39603142-4cc9-11ea-95a0-43d18ec715f5

Borgen Project (2020). *Five facts about healthcare in Romania.* Retrieved from https://borgenproject.org/healthcare-in-romania/

Central Statistical Office (Poland) (2013). *Informancja r rozmiarach I kierunkach emigracji z Polski w latach 2004–2012* [Information regarding the size and directions of emigration from Poland in 2004-2012]. Retrieved from https://stat.gov.pl/cps/rde/xbcr/gus/L_Szacunek_emigracji_z_Polski_lata_2004-2012_XI_2012.pdf

Centrum Badania Opinii Społecznej (2013). *Poakcesyjne Migracje Zarobkowe* [Post-accession economic migration]. Retrieved from https://www.cbos.pl/SPISKOM.POL/2013/K_166_13.PDF

Charmes, J. (2019). *The unpaid care work and the labour market. An analysis of time use data based on the latest world compilation of time-use surveys.* Geneva: ILO. Retrieved from https://www.ilo.org/wcmsp5/groups/public/---dgreports/---gender/documents/publication/wcms_732791.pdf

Council of Europe (2018). *European Commission for Democracy through Law (Venice Commission): Romania. Opinion on amendments to the Criminal Code and the Criminal Procedure Code, opinion No. 930/2018.* Retrieved from https://www.venice.coe.int/webforms/documents/default.aspx?pdffile=CDL-AD(2018)021-e

Eurofound (2021). *Living and working in Poland.* Retrieved from https://www.eurofound.europa.eu/country/poland

European Commission (20014). *Labour mobility within the EU.* Memo 25 September 2014. Retrieved from https://ec.europa.eu/commission/presscorner/detail/en/MEMO_14_541

European Commission (2019). *Rule of law: European Commission launches infringement procedures to protect judges in Poland from political control.* Retrieved from https://ec.europa.eu/commission/presscorner/detail/es/IP_19_1957

European Commission (2021a). *Infant mortality sharply declined over the past decades.* Retrieved from https://ec.europa.eu/eurostat/de/web/products-eurostat-news/product/-/asset_publisher/VWJkHuaYvLIN/content/id/12773418/pop_up

European Commission (2021b). *State of health in the EU: Romania. Country health profile 2021.* Retrieved from https://ec.europa.eu/health/sites/default/files/state/docs/2021_chp_romania_english.pdf

European Commission (n.d.). Romania–unemployment. Retrieved from https://ec.europa.eu/social/main.jsp?catId=1126&langId=en&intPageId=4758

European Institute for Gender Equality (2020a). *Gender Equality Index 2020: United*

Kingdom. Retrieved from https://eige.europa.eu/publications/gender-equality-index-2020-united-kingdom

European Institute for Gender Equality (2020b). *Gender Equality Index 2020 country fact sheet*. Retrieved from https://eige.europa.eu/areas/gender-equality-index-2020-country-factsheets

European Stability Initiative (2021). *How the rule of law dies in Poland*. Retrieved from https://www.esiweb.org/proposals/how-rule-law-dies-poland

Eurostat (2020). *EU Children at risk of poverty and social exclusion*. Retrieved from https://ec.europa.eu/eurostat/de/web/products-eurostat-news/-/ddn-20200305-1

Eurostat (2021a). *Mean and median income by household type*. Retrieved from https://www.ncbi.nlm.nih.gov/pmc/articles/PMC2855911/

Eurostat (2021b). *Mortality and life expectancy statistics*. Retrieved from https://ec.europa.eu/eurostat/statistics-explained/index.php?title=Mortality_and_life_expectancy_statistics#Life_expectancy_at_birth

Eurostat (2022a). *November 2021: Euro area unemployment at 7.2%*. Retrieved from https://ec.europa.eu/eurostat/documents/2995521/14084165/3-10012022-AP-EN.pdf/53ac483e-71d9-3093-5bd8-12f1ea89683a

Eurostat (2021c). *Social protection statistics – social benefits*. Retrieved from https://ec.europa.eu/eurostat/statistics-explained/index.php?title=Social_protection_statistics_-_social_benefits

Eurostat (2022b). *Mean and median income by household type–EU-SILC and ECHP surveys*. Retrieved from https://appsso.eurostat.ec.europa.eu/nui/show.do?dataset=ilc_di04

Fernandez-Reino, M. and Rienzo, C. (2022). Migrants in the UK Labour Market. *Migration Observatory*, 6 January 2022. Retrieved from https://migrationobservatory.ox.ac.uk/resources/briefings/migrants-in-the-uk-labour-market-an-overview/

Fries-Tersch, E., Jones, M. & Siöland, L. (2021). *Annual report on intra-EU labour mobility 2020*. Luxembourg: Publications Office of the European Union

Haivas, I. (2010). Health care in Romania: Fighting collapse. *Canadian Medial Association Journal, 182* (7): 654–655, https://www.ncbi.nlm.nih.gov/pmc/articles/PMC2855911/

Health Consumer Powerhouse (2019). *Euro health consumer index 2018*. Retrieved from https://healthpowerhouse.com/media/EHCI-2018/EHCI-2018-report.pdf

Jaźwińska-Motylska, E. (ed.) (2013). Kariery i mobilność społecznozawodowa migrantów poakcesyjnych [Careers and socio-professional mobility of post-accession migrants]. *CMR Working Papers, 65* (123). University of Warsaw, Centre of Migration Research (CMR), Warsaw

Kalfin, I. and Kyuchukov, L. (2018). *The Impact of labour migration on the Bulgarian economy*. Sophia; Friedrich Ebert Foundation. Retrieved from http://library.fes.de/pdf-files/bueros/sofia/15336-the_impact_of_labour_migration_on_the_bulgarian_economy.pdf

Mlady, M. (2005). Regional unemployment in the European Union and candidate countries in 2004. *Statistics in Focus, 3*(2005). Retrieved from *https://ec.europa.eu/eurostat/documents/3433488/5574884/KS-DN-05-003-EN.PDF.pdf/2b41f096-fbdd-46fe-9674-51e583dd6d46?t=1414693063000*

NHS (2005). *NHS Staff Earnings Survey–August 2004.* Retrieved from https://digital.nhs.uk/data-and-information/publications/statistical/nhs-staff-earnings/nhs-staff-earnings-survey-august-2004

OECD (n.d.a). *Closing the Gender Gap: Poland.* Retrieved from https://www.oecd.org/gender/Closing%20the%20Gender%20Gap%20-%20Poland%20FINAL.pdf

OECD (n.d.b). *Employment: Time spent in paid and unpaid work by sex.* Retrieved from https://stats.oecd.org/index.aspx?queryid=54757

OECD (2021). *Net replacement rate in unemployment.* Retrieved from https://stats.oecd.org/Index.aspx?DataSetCode=NRR

Office for National Statistics (2021a). *Healthcare expenditure, UK health accounts: 2019.* Retrieved from https://www.ons.gov.uk/peoplepopulationandcommunity/healthandsocialcare/healthcaresystem/bulletins/ukhealthaccounts/2019#:~:text=1.-,Main%20points,compared%20with%209.9%25%20in%202018

Office for National Statistics (2015). *Population by country of birth and nationality report: August 2015.* Retrieved from https://www.ons.gov.uk/peoplepopulationandcommunity/populationandmigration/internationalmigration/articles/populationbycountryofbirthandnationalityreport/2015-09-27

Office for National Statistics (2018). *Population of the UK by country of birth and nationality: 2017.* Retrieved from https://www.ons.gov.uk/peoplepopulationandcommunity/populationandmigration/internationalmigration/bulletins/ukpopulationbycountryofbirthandnationality/2017/previous/v

Office for National Statistics (2021b). *National life tables–life expectancy in the UK: 2018–2020.* Retrieved from https://www.ons.gov.uk/peoplepopulationandcommunity/birthsdeathsandmarriages/lifeexpectancies/bulletins/nationallifetablesunitedkingdom/2018to2020

Okólski, M. and Salt, J. (2014). Polish emigration to the UK after 2004: Why did so many come? *Central and Eastern European Migration Review,* December 2014, 1–27

Reporters Without Borders (2021a). *Poland.* Retrieved from https://rsf.org/en/poland

Reporters Without Borders (2021b). *RFS declares 'press freedom state of emergency'.* 13 September 2021. Retrieved from https://rsf.org/en/news/rsf-declares-press-freedom-state-emergency-poland

Rettmann, A. (2019). Romania warned of EU wrath over corruption. *EU Observer,* 14 May 2019. Retrieved from https://euobserver.com/justice/144887

Romania Insider (2019). Health minister: 25,000 doctors left Romania in the last ten years. *Romania Insider,* 18 December 2019. Retrieved from https://www.romania-insider.com/index.php/health-minister-doctors-left-romania

Statista (2021). *Employment rate of UK and non-UK born adults in the United Kingdom from 1st quarter 1997 to 3rd quarter 2021.* Retrieved from https://www.statista.com/statistics/915732/immigrant-employment-rate-uk/

Statista (2022a). *Average net monthly salary in Romania from 1989 to 2021 (in Romanian lei)*. Retrieved from https://www.statista.com/statistics/1261244/romania-average-net-monthly-salary/

Statista (2022b). *Number of Polish nationals resident in the United Kingdom from 2008 to 2021*. Retrieved from https://www.statista.com/statistics/1061639/polish-population-in-united-kingdom/

Statistics Poland (2018). Average monthly gross wage and salary in national economy 1950-2020. Retrieved from https://stat.gov.pl/en/topics/labour-market/working-employed-wages-and-salaries-cost-of-labour/average-monthly-gross-wage-and-salary-in-national-economy-1950-2020,2,1.html

Statistisches Bundesamt (2022). *EU November 2021: EU unemployment rate at 6.5%*. Retrieved from https://www.destatis.de/Europa/EN/Topic/Population-Labour-Social-Issues/Labour-market/EULabourMarketCrisis.html

The Greens/EFA (2018). *The cost of corruption across the EU*. Retrieved from https://www.greens-efa.eu/files/doc/docs/e46449daadbfebc325a0b408bbf5ab1d.pdf

The World Bank (2021a). *GDP per capita (current US$): Poland*. Retrieved from https://data.worldbank.org/indicator/NY.GDP.PCAP.CD?locations=PL

The World Bank (2021b). *GDP per capita (current US$): United Kingdom*. Retrieved from https://data.worldbank.org/indicator/NY.GDP.PCAP.CD?locations=GB Statista (2021)

Transparency International (2021). *Corruption Perceptions Index 2020*. https://images.transparencycdn.org/images/CPI2020_Report_EN_0802-WEB-1_2021-02-08-103053.pdf

Vargas-Silva, C. (2014). EU Migration to the UK: Trends and impacts. *Intereconomics, 49* (3), 116–158. Retrieved from https://www.intereconomics.eu/contents/year/2014/number/3/article/labour-mobility-in-the-eu-dynamics-patterns-and-policies.html

Vargas-Silva, C., and Walsh, P. (2020). *EU migration to and from the UK*. Migration Observatory, 2 October 2020. Retrieved from https://migrationobservatory.ox.ac.uk/resources/briefings/eu-migration-to-and-from-the-uk/

Warsaw Institute (2018). *How will Brexit affect Romanian health care workers in the UK?* Retrieved from https://warsawinstitute.org/will-brexit-affect-romanian-health-care-workers-uk/

Watt, N. and Wintour, P. (2015). How immigration came to haunt Labour: the inside story. *The Guardian*. Retrieved from https://www.theguardian.com/news/2015/mar/24/how-immigration-came-to-haunt-labour-inside-story

GERMANY:

III

Why does Germany have so many refugees from the Middle East?

Abstract   The civil war in Syria has been one of the biggest humanitarian tragedies in modern history, with over 400,000 people dead and another 13.5 million–close to two thirds of the Syrian population–forcibly displaced, domestically and internationally, since 2011. The international community was put under considerable pressure to provide adequate support for the millions of refugees who arrived in neighbouring Lebanon, Turkey, at the shores of Greece, and in central Europe. Yet, the unprecedented scale of the Syrian refugee crisis meant that immediate responses were not always adequate. This was particularly evident in the EU, which received 2.5 million asylum applications in 2015 and 2016 alone. Due to a lack of agreement among the European community, there exists a big imbalance regarding the number of accepted refugees, with Germany granting asylum to around half of the one million Syrian refugees that arrived in the EU between 2011 and 2017 (Connor, 2018). This chapter analyses the reasons why so many people fleeing Syria (and also Iraq and Afghanistan) ended up in Germany, looking at both pull factors that attracted the refugees to Germany and the nation's policies that welcomed Middle Eastern asylum seekers.

What this chapter covers: Asylum, refugees, EU refugee policy, German social security, welcome culture in the EU, European responses to refugees 2015/2016, Syria, Iraq, public opinion on refugees

Introduction

"Wir schaffen das" ("We can do it"). This is how then Chancellor Angela Merkel of Germany addressed her people on August 31st, 2015 in light of the surge of refugees from the Middle East. 'It' refers to accepting (and integrating) the tens of thousands of asylum seekers that had already reached Germany by that point as well as the many more eagerly waiting to seek asylum in Europe's biggest nation. Due to the raging civil war in Syria, the number of asylum seekers spiralled, with Germany registering well over a thousand daily new arrivals in the autumn of 2015. While Hungary, under Prime Minister Viktor Orbán, closed its borders relatively early, installing wire fences at its border with Serbia and Croatia in June 2015, Angela Merkel decided to keep Germany open. As a result, over 1,500 asylum seekers reached Munich Central Station alone by train from Vienna and Budapest daily in September 2015. Many of them were welcomed by cheering volunteers who donated food, drinks, clothes, and sanitary products.

This chapter assesses why so many refugees from Syria and Iraq applied for asylum in Germany rather than in EU member states much closer to their home country, such as Greece, Bulgaria, Hungary, or Croatia. To understand the refugees' motivation, we will look at the support systems for asylum seekers in several EU countries, their general living conditions in different member states, the different acceptance rates of asylum applications, public opinion on refugees in diverse countries, and familiarity with Germany among Syrian and Iraqi refugees. In addition, we will also analyse the 'supply side', namely German policies that attracted and welcomed over a million asylum seekers in just a few years.

We will show that, while the reasons are manifold for why around half of all EU-bound refugees from Syria found a new home in Germany, its high acceptance of applications and generous financial benefits for asylum seekers were the main factors for Germany's popularity, next to the country's good economic situation and thriving labour market.

In the following, we will look at the definitions of refugees and asylum seekers, assessing what makes someone qualify as a refugee, and discuss their rights, as well the extent to which different EU countries have supported them.

> As of late 2019, Germany was home to nearly 1.5 million refugees and asylum seekers–raising their share to about 1.2% of the overall population. While Sweden, on a per capita basis, has an even higher share of refugees and asylum seekers, German acceptance of refugees from the Middle East remains unmatched in Europe. About half of all refugees and asylum seekers in Germany are from Syria.

> Despite the overwhelmingly positive reaction among the German population in 2015, criticism regarding Merkel's crisis management became more widespread in subsequent years. Due to the high costs associated with housing and integrating asylum seekers and the fear that accepting more than one million Muslim refugees could lead to a loss of German national identity and cause a rise in terrorism and violent crime, voices that condemned Merkel's open-door policy became more frequent. Thus, her slogan "We can do it" and the acceptance of millions of asylum seekers quickly became the most controversial decision during her 16-year career as German chancellor.

What are refugees and asylum seekers, and what rights do they have?

What makes people leave their home country? Simply put, it is the hope for a better life. For most refugees, this implies a life free from persecution and war, and, by extension, a safe home or shelter. Unlike economic migrants, who usually leave their home country to find wealth and higher living standards in a new country, refugees flee their motherland to save their lives. But what exactly makes a person a refugee? The 1951 Refugee Convention defines a refugee as someone who has left his or her country of origin "owing to a well-founded fear of being persecuted for reasons of race, religion, nationality, membership of a particular social group, or political opinion" (UNHCR, n.d.) In other words, refugees are usually people who have fled war, violence, and persecution at home, and seek shelter in a foreign country.

The 148 countries that either signed the Convention Relating to the Status of Refugees from 1951 (better known as 1951 Refugee Convention, or the Geneva Convention of 28 July 1951) or the 1967 Protocol are obliged to accept refugees and to enable them a life in safety. The rights of asylum seekers, as well the responsibilities of the signatory nations that grant asylum (as described in the 1951 Refugee Convention) are as follows: in addition to providing free access to courts for refugees (Article 16), administrative assistance for refugees (Article 25), identity papers for refugees (Article 27), travel documents for refugees (Article 28) and the possibility of assimilation and naturalisation to refugees (Article 34), countries should ensure that refugees are not discriminated against and receive the same treatment, social benefits and access to education and the labour force as either nationals or other foreigners in the country (UNHR, n.d.) In other words, refugees should have the freedom to work, move, and receive education. In order for refugees to live normally, states are expected to support them economically and socially. This means that asylum seekers (refugees whose status is not yet determined) generally have the right to receive housing assistance (either in form of the provision of housing or housing subsidies), financial support to buy food and other daily necessities, and access to medical care and schooling. Once asylum seekers are granted refugee status (which means their application was accepted), they have the same rights as nationals or other legally residing foreigners regarding access to the labour market and social security systems. The equal treatment of approved refugees to nationals is also defined in the 1951 Refugee Convention, which proposes that "[r]efugees shall be treated at least like nationals in relation to freedom to practice their religion (Article 4), elementary education (Article 22), public relief and assistance (Article 23) and labour legislation and social security (Article 24)."

Different states use different measures to assess whether the person reaching their territory should be treated as a refugee. As previously mentioned, refugees are people who have a "well-founded fear of being persecuted for reasons of race, religion, nationality, membership of a particular social group, or political opinion", which makes them unable or unwilling to return to their home country. Yet, how do we assess what qualifies as a well-founded fear? The vagueness of the definition lies at the core of why different countries grant refuge to different people, and why acceptance rates vary so greatly. In Japan, for example, less than 1% of all asylum seekers are granted refugee status every year. This is mainly due to the country's strict national asylum regulations that stand in stark contrast to many European nations or the United States, which have acceptance rates of 30% to 40%, on average. While in Japan, 19,628 people applied for asylum in 2017, only 20 (around 0.1%) were granted asylum and given refugee status (Reuters, 2018). In 2016, the year Germany granted asylum to 263,622 out of the 745,545 applicants, Japan gave asylum to 28 people (out of 10,901 applications), making the recognition rate 34% vs. 0.25%, respectively (Berman, 2018). Germany's high recognition rate of asylum seekers made it not only the number one country in terms of applications for asylum received among all G-20 nations, but also the European leader in terms of acceptance rate. While Germany granted asylum to 34% of all applicants in 2016, the UK had a recognition rate of 29%, France of 18%, Italy of 5%, Spain of 4% and Hungary of 0.28% (Berman, 2018).

Although the term refugee is commonly used to refer to someone fleeing their country because of war or persecution, the political definition of a refugee is an asylum seeker whose application has been accepted and refugee status granted. Whether they are accepted as refugees lies in the hands of the governments of the respective countries, which assess asylum applications. As it takes considerable time to analyse all the documents and personal backgrounds of asylum seekers–in many cases, interviews have to be conducted to assess whether the person is truly persecuted in his/her home country and cannot be protected by their own government–asylum is usually only granted after several months of waiting. As asylum seekers often do not apply immediately for asylum when entering the new country, the time from arrival to a final decision can take up to two years.

During the time asylum seekers are waiting for a decision on their status, they receive physical protection as well as monetary support from the host country. Most receive housing in public or private units or rent support, furniture, and subsidies for food (or cooked meals), as well as financial assistance for telecommunication, transport, education, and hobbies. In addition, they should have free access to education, health care, and courts. However, before being granted refugee status, they cannot legally work in the recipient country.

When refugees reach foreign shores, they often do not have much more than what they are wearing, in addition to limited funds. For many, the journey to a safe country is long and exhausting and takes a physical, emotional, and financial toll. Thus, countries are expected to provide not only a safe home, but also emotional, social, and financial support to asylum seekers. To what extent, and in what form states should support asylum seekers is, however, not set in the 1951 Refugee Convention or other international agreements. As such, considerable variation exists among states regarding the scope of financial and social support. Due to the stark differences in how states treat refugees and what they offer (in addition to their geographical location), the number of asylum applications submitted in different EU states varies starkly. In fact, many refugees engage in the (illegal) practice of 'asylum shopping and do not apply for asylum in the state where they first reached the EU (as required by the Dublin Regulation), but transition to other member states to apply for asylum in the state they want to live in–a decision also based on the amount of (financial) support granted by the individual states. We will discuss this in depth when assessing why so many asylum seekers have chosen Germany as their destination.

Why does Germany have so many asylum seekers?

Looking at how refugees are spread across the EU, one notices a strong imbalance among the member states. Just six countries–

Germany, Hungary, Sweden, Austria, Germany, France and Italy–, out of which three have a population of under 10 million, received over 80% of all asylum applications in 2015 (Altmeyer-Bartscher et al., 2016). If we look at the number of asylum permits granted, the picture is just as unequal, with Germany alone hosting around half of all Syrian refugees in the EU. Many countries, especially in eastern Europe, in contrast, have given asylum to an incredibly small number of people arriving from the Middle East.

Why does such an imbalance exist? A major reason for the high number of people who initially applied for refuge in Greece and Hungary in 2015 were geographical factors. Hungary was the first point of contact with the EU for the over a million people who reached the EU through the 'Balkan route', making their way from Iraq and Syria over land and entered Hungary from Serbia. Thus, it is rather self-explicatory that Hungary received a high volume of asylum seekers from Iraq and Syria in 2015 and 2016. Greece was similarly a first point of contact for many who tried to enter the EU by boat.

According to the Dublin Convention, asylum seekers must remain in the country where they first entered the EU and are obliged to register or get fingerprinted there immediately. The agreement further stipulates that asylum seekers can be sent back to the country where they entered the EU (or where they were first recorded). With this regulation in mind, how can it be that Germany and Sweden, two countries right in the middle of Europe with no external borders to non-EU/EEA countries, have the highest number of refugees in absolute figures and per capita, respectively? The only legitimate reasons to claim asylum in Germany or Sweden would be that the person arrived directly by plane or boat. However, this is very unlikely, as the Baltic and North Sea are neither part of the migrant routes, nor can large numbers of asylum seekers board a plane to Germany or Sweden without a valid visa. Thus, most of the over 1.3 million asylum seekers that arrived in Sweden and Germany in 2015 and 2016 must have failed to register and remain in the country where they first entered the EU. This phenomenon of refugees not staying in the country where they entered the EU is, as described above, against EU law, and this practice of 'asylum shopping' (trying to reach another country to maximise their benefits) makes some of the asylum seekers de-facto economic migrants.

However, the asylum seekers are not the only ones to blame. Countries like Hungary were often reluctant to fingerprint and register incoming asylum seekers, as this reduced their obligation to start the asylum process for those entering and made it harder for other countries to return asylum seekers. By not registering a large number of asylum seekers, Hungary, for example, was hoping that the majority of new arrivals from Syria and Iraq would leave for wealthier, more generous EU member states to apply for asylum there. And they were right: many asylum seekers who entered the EU through Hungary took the train from Budapest to Vienna and Munich to seek asylum in Germany, Austria, or Sweden.

Despite the unequal distribution of refugees and asylum seekers across the EU, many member states–especially those spared by masses of asylum applications, such as most eastern Countries–have been reluctant to accept refugees from other EU member states. When the EU proposed a redistribution scheme where the countries most overwhelmed with asylum seekers, such as Greece and Italy, should be allowed to reallocate some of their refugees to other EU member states, four eastern EU countries states (Hungary, Slovakia, the Czech Republic, and Romania) voted against this decision. Hungary and Slovakia went as far as to challenge the decision on relocation of refugees at the European Court of Justice (Šabić, 2017). Although their case was unsuccessful, many eastern European countries have refrained from accepting relocated refugees from other EU states. As a result, out of the envisaged 98,255 resettlements, fewer than 30,000 took place, both due to resistance from different EU member states and from among the refugees themselves, who were against being sent to countries with less generous social security benefits and lower living standards (Šabić, 2017). In the end, ironically, it were often countries that already had high numbers of refugees, such as Germany, that accepted relocations from other EU member states, increasing their burden even further. This reveals a lack of solidarity and the free-rider phenomenon among several EU member states, which contributed very little to asylum protection but benefitted from other states taking in most refugees.

When asylum seekers choose their destination, their decision is often based on rationality. Questions they might ask themselves include: where will I have a good life? Where do I get the most support? Where are people most welcoming? Where do I already know people? Where exists a large minority from my country? Where am I treated with respect? Where can a find a job most easily afterwards? Where are my chances of being accepted the highest? Where can I receive sufficient financial and housing support for a life in dignity? For many asylum seekers, the answers to these questions are often not eastern European countries or Greece, where support is often limited due to economic restrains, where the general population is often against refugees, and where the acceptance rates are low. For many, countries with generous welfare systems, a functioning labour market, a strong economy, protection of human rights, and a high acceptance rate are more highly favoured. One such country is Germany.

In the following, we will assess the pull factors that attract asylum seekers to Germany, starting with the high acceptance rate and the duration for which their stay is permitted.

1) High acceptance rate of asylum seekers

According to EU law, asylum seekers can only apply for asylum in one EU member state. If the result of their application is negative, they are not allowed to apply for asylum anywhere else in the EU. Thus, it is important for many asylum seekers to choose a country with a high acceptance rate. Germany has one of the highest acceptance rates in the EU; in 2015, over 95% of all asylum seekers from Iraq and over 97% from Syria received refugee status, which came with an initial three-year residence permit (Burmann/Valeyatheepillay, 2017). While the acceptance rate of Syrians subsequently dropped from 97.4% to 57.2% between 2015 and 2016, Germany still accepted more asylum seekers–both in absolute figures and in regard to the application rate–than all its EU neighbours.

Whilst all EU member states follow the Geneva Convention and the Common European Asylum System, which require them to take in refugees, their national policies regarding accepting and supporting refugees vary massively. How the criteria set by EU member states regarding the acceptance of refugees differ can be seen best in the following statistics on how many granted refugee status to asylum seekers from Iraq and Syria in 2015. In Germany, where the government considered the civil war in Iraq and Syria a major threat to human life, the acceptance rate of Iragi asylum seekers was 95.7%, and Syria 97.4% for Syrians. The same year, asylum seekers from Iraq and Syria only had a 19.8% and 42.7% chance of being accepted in Italy. While this rose to 92.8% the year after for Syrians (due to a new government policy on Syrian refugees), the acceptance rate for Iraqis remained low (Burmann/Valeyatheepillay, 2017). In Hungary, the rates for Syrian asylum seekers were even considerably lower, standing at 5.7%. While the acceptance rate in Hungary was already low in 2015–with around 19 times fewer successful applications than in Germany–, the soaring numbers of asylum seekers reaching the borders of Hungary from Serbia in 2015 led to a legislative change that made Hungary less attractive as destination for refugees and allowed it to reject more applications. Since the completion of Hungary's new wire fence border to Serbia and Croatia in September 2015, Hungary "claims to have rejected all asylum requests at their border" and announced that those trespassing into Hungary might have to pay for the costs associated with their detention. All these measures not only reduced asylum claims in Hungary but also lowered the acceptance rate of Syrian asylum seekers to 0.5% in 2016 (Burmann/Valeyatheepillay, 2017).

This shows that the different acceptance rates among EU states can be traced back to two major reasons: the nationality of the applicants (in countries where many Syrians applied for asylum, the rate tends to be higher as most were granted asylum to the on-going civil war in their country), and the openness of national immigration regimes. In many eastern European countries, governments have been much less permissive in regard to asylum seekers, setting high hurdles for successful applications. In many EU-15 nations, in contrast, governments have a more liberal approach to the immigration of refugees. When determining whether asylum should be granted, EU governments apply different methods and evaluation tools, which often depend on their general stance on immigration.

It is fair to assume that those fleeing war and prosecution in Syria and Iraq were probably not aware of the exact acceptance rates in different EU countries, but they had probably heard that most applicants were successful in Germany while Hungary, for example, rejected most applications. Thus, the high acceptance rate for Syrian and Iraqi asylum seekers can be regarded as one of the reasons why so many of them choose to apply for asylum in Germany.

> Application success around the world: while countries like Japan and South Korea, for example, set very high hurdles for asylum seekers to be accepted, Germany, the US and Canada tend to be more permissive.

2) Generous financial support for asylum seekers

In order to live a life in dignity, asylum seekers, no matter the stage of their application, receive government funding in most EU countries. However, the amount of money received varies greatly among EU member states, with countries like Hungary or Bulgaria providing very little financial support. Similarly, most refugees arriving in Turkey receive little or no money from the government to assist them with daily necessities. Thus, asylum seekers often try to reach countries where the expected benefits are high and there are good support systems in place. In Germany, asylum seekers receive financial assistance in forms of goods and cash transfers. In 2015, 91% of all asylum seekers in Germany received the standard financial assistance, which comprised of cash transfers of around €350 per person, in addition to housing (or financial subsidies for housing), payment of utility bills, and furniture (Destatis, 2016). Already by the end of 2015, close to 1 million people received the aforementioned assistance, which was guaranteed by the Asylum Seekers Benefits Act (*Asylbewerberleistungsgesetz*, or AsylbLG for short). Once the application for asylum is granted, refugees no longer receive social assistance under the Asylum Seekers Benefits Act but can access any social welfare fund that is open to Germans, e.g., Hartz IV if they are unemployed or on a low income. In addition to the standard financial assistance and the housing subsidies, around 340,000 asylum seekers received further special needs financial support–mainly due to illness, pregnancy, or childbirth–in 2015 (Destatis, 2016). In 2016, these cash and non-cash payments to asylum seekers by the German federal states under the Asylum Seekers Benefits Act amounted to approximately €9.2 billion–a considerable sum (Bundeszentrale für politische Bildung, 2020). When assessing the overall asylum-related expenditure by the German federal government, the figure reached €23 billion for 2018, or around 7% of the total state budget. It includes not only direct transfers in goods and cash to asylum seekers but also payments to the 16 federal states to cover parts of their expenditure for housing and supporting asylum seekers, administrative costs, federal housing expenses in the initial stage of their application, and measures to integrate asylum seekers and refugees, as well as payments to countries like Turkey for hosting refugees, or payments to failing states to reduce the causes of flight and to limit future waves of asylum seekers. As Germany has a population of roughly 82 million people, the central governments' expenditures for asylum seekers and refugees alone amounted to approximately €280 per person in 2018.

If we compare the financial support refugees receive in different EU member states, it becomes apparent that Germany is one of the most generous countries. The €354 (plus rent subsidies and non-cash transfers) provided to asylum seekers in private accommodation in 2018 is considerably more generous than in many other countries, even those with a strong welfare system, such as Sweden, where asylum seekers in private accommodation receive around €225 each month, in addition to subsidies covering rent and utilities.[1] In France, the monthly allowance amounts to €202 per

---

[1] In 2021, the basic financial assistance for asylum seekers in Germany amounted to €364 per month, in addition to housing and other non-cash transfers. In case two people live together in one household (e.g. as married couple) or for people living in state accommodation, the standard rate is reduced by 10%, to €328 per month, in addition to non-financial support. The same is true for teenagers aged 15 to 18. Not married children under 25 who live with their parents receive €292, with smaller children receiving slightly less (€247 or €282, depending on their age).

person, with every subsequent member in the household receiving half of that. However, only people in shared state accommodation are eligible for this support. If asylum seekers refuse to live in such state-run centres, they lose their right for financial assistance. The same is true for Italy, where only those in official group homes (reception centres) receive financial support of €75 a month (plus food, hygiene products and clothing) for each unemployed adult asylum seeker (Hodali/Prange, 2018).

If we look at monetary benefits for adults in state-run group homes, we find that Germany is the clear leader in regard to cash payments. Every single adult in such homes received €135 per month for private expenses, with food, housing and utilities paid for separately. This is considerably higher than France's €75, Sweden's €70, Spain's €50 and Austria's €40. Also in regard to payments to minors or partners living together, the German allowances are considerably higher, with small children receiving over €200 in private accommodation–much more than the UK's €13 per month for children under three, or Spain's allowance of €19 for children in group homes (Hodali/Prange, 2018).

Why is the financial assistance so different among the EU member states, although all of them follow the 1951 Geneva Convention and the Common European Asylum System? The main reason is that there is no European or international standard regarding how much support states should grant asylum seekers. Also, the EU promulgation that states should secure "adequate standard of living for applicants, which guarantees their subsistence and protects their physical and mental health" is interpreted very differently. How much asylum seekers receive mainly depends on national legislation. In many cases, states with a strong welfare system allocate higher funding for asylum seekers and refugees. In Germany, for example, the financial assistance for asylum seekers is just slightly below state support for those on social benefits (Hartz IV).

While people fleeing their home country are probably not aware of the exact regulations and financial support in each EU member state, the internet has made it easy for them to receive information regarding which countries treat asylum seekers with respect, as well as how generously new arrivals are supported. In Germany, during the height of the 'refugee crisis', the federal states built hundreds of new group homes to house the refugees. Pictures of their brand-new rooms, as well photos of them holding the cash payments from the government in their hands, quickly spread online and 'invited' more people to seek refuge in Germany rather than in other countries.

3) Welcoming population

The power of pictures also becomes evident when analysing to what extent a welcoming population contributed to Germany's asylum seeker population. It was not only the selfie of young asylum seeker Anas Modamani posing with then Chancellor Angela Merkel that went viral, but also pictures of Germans holding up posters with 'refugees welcome' and of volunteers hugging the newly arrived refugees at Munich Central Station. This welcoming, open atmosphere in Germany (for which soon a new term–*Willkommenskultur*, or welcome culture–was coined), which was especially prevalent in 2015 and 2016, contributed to asylum seekers' desire to move to Germany rather than other countries. It also might have convinced those with no clear intention as to where they wanted to reside in Europe not to remain in Greece or Hungary, the countries of first contact with the EU, but to move on towards Germany. When comparing public attitudes towards refugees in Hungary and in Greece with that of Germany, it becomes clear that a lack of people making them feel welcome, especially in Hungary (but also in the many refugee camps on Greek islands), also contributed to refugees moving further west.

Assessing public opinion regarding refugees in different EU member states makes it obvious that the German population was among the most positive. A 2017 survey by the Bertelsmann Foundation (2017) conducted among people aged 15 to 24 in six European countries revealed that, while 73% of young Germans agreed that their country should accept refugees, the vast majority in Poland, Slovakia, the Czech Republic and Hungary opposed such a decision, ranging from 70% in the Czech Republic to 73% in Poland.

Only in Austria was a small majority (61%) of youngsters also in favour of granting asylum. A study by the Pew Research Center from spring 2018 shows that even after the EU had received over 1.3 million refugees in 2015 and 2016, the vast majority of people (79%–86%) in Spain, the Netherlands, Germany, Sweden and France supported the idea that their government should take in "refugees from countries where people are fleeing violence and war". The majority of people in Poland and Hungary opposed this (Poushter, 2016). Similarly, 64%–73% of people in Greece, Hungary and Italy saw refugees from Syria and Iraq as a major threat, while only 24% of Swedish, 31% of German and 36% of Dutch people agreed with this statement. This reveals that in central European countries with a strong economy, a generous welfare state and a multicultural society (e.g. Germany, Sweden, Austria and the Netherlands), public opinion towards refugees tended to be welcoming and supportive, while especially in the ethnically more homogenous eastern European member states, the general public was largely against accepting asylum seekers.

In the second half of 2015 and in 2016, hundreds of thousands of volunteers and NGOs in different (mainly EU-15) member states organised support for the refugees reaching their countries. Examples include 2,200 Austrians driving all the way to Budapest to pick up stranded refugees and taking them to Austria, and people in Munich providing so much food, refreshments, clothes, and sanitary products in September 2015 that the police, overwhelmed by all the donations, even ordered people to stop bringing more. In many more countries (Denmark and Sweden are some examples), locals donated food and clothes to the new arrivals and helped them settle into their new home country. Frykman and Mäkelä (2019) describe how, in Sweden, volunteers welcomed refugees in Malmö with refreshments, food, clothes and money for their onward journey or for accommodation for the night. Similarly, German volunteers, often united by the 'Refugees Welcome' movement, offered the arrivals both temporary and long-term support in regard to integration, learning the language, and settling into German society. Although voices against accepting more refugees became stronger in many EU countries over the years, mainly as a response to the unprecedented scale of incoming asylum seekers in 2015, 2016 and

2017, German public opinion remained largely supportive. Unlike in several other EU member states, a considerable number of Germans have actively been involved in supporting refugees from Syria and Iraq, with many NGOs still helping to integrate refugees today.

Thus, the welcoming culture and the supportive, open attitude of most Germans could be one factor that attracted asylum seekers to Germany or made them stay there after arrival.

4) Favourable living conditions and positive economic situation of the recipient country

Another factor that might have contributed to many asylum seekers applying for refugee status in Germany could be the country's favourable living conditions. Unlike in Greece, where they were usually housed in temporary camps, sometimes without sufficient food, sanitation, heating, or clothes, many refugees in Germany lived in relatively new, properly constructed group homes. As Greece was surprised by the surge of asylum seekers from Syria in 2015 and 2016, the government started to erect over two-dozen camps to temporarily house them. The most famous camp, Moria, on the island of Lesbos, soon became a symbol of the Greek (and European) failure to cope with the high influx of asylum seekers. Built originally for around 3,000 people, the camp soon housed 20,000 refugees, who often lived in unsanitary conditions in overcrowded tents. While the situation was difficult for nearly all residents, the 6,000 to 7,000 children under 18 in particular suffered from these unhygienic, cramped conditions. While Moria is typically referred to as a tent camp, many residents lived in very basic, makeshift accommodations built in an olive grove next to the original camp. Much of the basic housing in this 'Moria jungle' was made from simple wooden pallets and tarps. Due to their abysmal living conditions, Moria was referred to as "the words refugee camp on Earth" by a field coordinator of Doctors Without Borders, who told the BBC that he had "never seen the level of suffering we are witnessing here every day" (Nye, 2018).

These living conditions stand in stark contrast with those in Germany, for example, where dozens of hotels were converted into group homes for refugees, and where the state spent several hundred million euro on constructing new housing for asylum seekers. While in Greece, people were often living in outside tents, in overcrowded, unhygienic conditions, asylum seekers in Germany were often housed in relatively spacious accommodation (a minimum of 6–7m² per person is suggested in Germany), with rent, heating and utilities paid for, and meals often provided. In addition, German asylum seekers received cash transfers, coupons or good to cover their daily expenditures and were offered intensive, free German language classes and integration courses. This is perhaps the biggest reason for why many asylum seekers who entered the EU through Greece (illegally) left the peninsula to make their way to Germany. Even among those who have remained in Greek camps, thousands hope to be relocated to Germany, either under the EU asylum seeker transfer mechanism or for family reunification. For many refugees, Greek camps feel "like a prison" (according to different sources), and many long for the day when they can be transferred to another country– ideally one with more generous welfare, a stronger economy, and better refugee management.

There are two main reasons why the situation in Greek camps is dismal. First, Greece received an unprecedented number of refugees in 2015 and was unprepared for such as 'storm' of new arrivals. In 2015 alone, over 850,000 refugees crossed the sea from Turkey to Greece to be stranded on islands or the mainland in need of housing. By mid-March 2016, the number of refugees who had arrived in Greece since 2015 even surpassed 1,000,0000. While the UNHCR (the UN Refugee Agency) and the European Union supported Greece financially and often also built their own camps or provided tents and other goods, the Greek government was unable to keep up with the rising demand. This was not only because of the sheer amount of people who arrived but also because Greece itself was in the middle of a major economic crisis and had little financial means to support the incoming refugees.

The wealth of a country is often reflected in the condition of housing and support for refugees, and that plays a major role for asylum seekers when deciding their preferred new home. While it is not legal for asylum seekers to leave the country where they were first registered or fingerprinted without a government permit (as this makes them economic migrants 'shopping' for better treatment), it happens relatively frequently. Similarly, the vast majority of refugees from Syria, Afghanistan, Pakistan and Iraq who arrived in Greece in 2015 failed to apply for asylum in the country: while around 800,000 refugees reached Greece in 2015, only 13,197 people applied for asylum there. A Flash Report by the European Commission proposes this is because "the majority of these people do not want to stay in Greece, a country [...] with a weak and ineffective welfare state and a staggering unemployment rate" (Sakellis et al., 2016).

The economic condition of a country also plays a role in regard to future employment opportunities. In Greece, for example, where unemployment rates skyrocketed between 2010 and 2016, the chances of refugees finding (well-paid) jobs are meagre. In Germany (as well as in several other EU states such as the Netherlands, Austria, and Sweden), unemployment rates are low, with ample jobs in all sectors and for all skill levels. While refugees only have a right to stay in the country that provides asylum for as long as it is not safe to return to their home country, many refugees hope to be able to stay in their new county of residence for longer. Thus, the conditions of the labour market and the chance to find employment also play a role when deciding where to move. The German labour market has been very favourable for years–a fact widely published and known around the world–so it is not unlikely that Syrian and Iraqi refugees factored in their future employment chances when making a decision.

Housing conditions and future employment opportunities play a vital role for refugees when selecting their desired country of destination. The internet allows refugees to get direct insights into how most refugees are hosted and treated in different countries, which helps them make a decision. While international systems state that the first safe country refugees reach should host them, many asylum seekers pick their destination based on the potential future living conditions in prospective countries. In many respects, asylum seekers hope to optimise the outcome of their decisions by making informed choices.

5) Familiarity with the country and existing contacts

Up to now, we have mainly looked at rational choice among refugees regarding their decision to move to Germany. However, one should not forget that people make decisions not only based on 'hard facts' and that they are not always predominantly motivated by monetary gains and maximisation of benefits. 'Soft' factors most likely played a role, too. One such factor could be a higher degree of familiarity with Germany–the biggest country in Europe in terms of population, the strongest economy in the EU, and one of the world's biggest exporters–than with other, smaller European countries such as Denmark, Luxembourg, Belgium, or the Netherlands. While the aforementioned countries have similarly generous welfare Systems and a per capita GDP around that of Germany's, these countries might have not been well known among refugees, which potentially reduced their interest. Studies have shown that humans, in general, opt for something they know, which could be one reason why so many of the people fleeing war in Iraq and Syria hoped to go to the country they might have heard of the most in the media: Germany.

Similar to having heard of or possessing some knowledge about Germany, knowing people in the country could have also played a major role for some refugees. Many foreigners–and refugees in particular–feel like outsiders in a country that is not their own and where they do not speak the language. Thus, there is a common phenomenon among migrants to choose a country where they already have family or friends, or at least acquaintances. The hurdle for people to choose an unknown country where they do not know a single person (or have not heard of anyone emigrating there) is high, which could explain why many asylum seekers from Iraq and Syria chose Germany, a country hosting already hundreds of thousands with the same nationality. Most refugees reaching Germany must have known someone who already lived there or who made their way to Germany before them. For many refugees who lost their home and sometimes also their family, being in a place with people from the same ethnic background would be important and explains why Germany has been the top choice among the majority of refugees from Iraq and Syria after 2015.

Why did Germany welcome so many refugees with open arms?

Although we have primarily focused on the motivations of Iraqis and Syrians in choosing Germany as their new country of residence, it is also important to consider the country's openness and welcoming attitude. In other words, to answer our research question, we should also ask ourselves "Why did Germany welcome so many refugees with open arms?" as this be another jigsaw piece to reach a conclusion. Had Germany closed its borders in September 2015 or had the overall German population vehemently opposed asylum seekers, it would be hard to imagine that over one million refugees would have reached the country and registered in just two years.

There are several reasons why Germany was open for receiving refugees. In the following, we will outline some of the most common:

- German guilt and shame regarding WWII, and the view among many people that Germany has to do good deeds, and thus cannot close its borders to those in need.
- A strong economy around 2015/16, which made many Germans believe that, while it would take a huge financial toll, they could afford to help as a country (in contrast to many other EU states, which still suffered from the effects of the previous financial crisis).
- The existence of a multicultural society (with about a quarter of the German population coming from a migrant background), due to which many Germans are more open to immigrants and asylum seekers than more ethnically homogeneous countries.
- An ageing society, a low birth rate, and rising labour shortages in some professions. Several academics and politicians argued that accepting refugees could support the German economy long-term, helping the country to fill its labour shortages and decrease the average age of the population.

In addition, some people propose that Chancellor Merkel's strong Christian ethics and her own personal morals forbade her from closing the borders to refugees. Had she reacted differently, and had she not convinced the German population that 'we can do it', fewer asylum seekers might have reached Germany and there could have been more resistance regarding support for the country's over 1.5 million asylum seekers and refugees since 2015.

All these factors also contributed to Germany becoming the EU's main country of destination for asylum seekers since 2015.

Conclusion

It is never easy to explain the decision of millions of people, not only because the reasons are so diverse, but also because, in many cases, even the individuals themselves do not exactly understand what triggered their decisions. The same is true for asylum seekers heading for Germany after 2015: many of them had no clear idea of what Germany was like or why they had decided to head there. Many of them might have been familiar with the country or had at least heard of it in the media; some might have been aware that Germany was a relatively wealthy country and offered comfortable housing for asylum seekers. Others might have seen pictures of asylum seekers in Germany who were holding up the euro bills they had received from the government to support their livelihood, while others might have been impressed by rumours that all taxis in Germany are supposedly Mercedes Benz. Yet others might have been aware that the country's population and politicians seemed to be more favourable to refugees than in other countries. Some people might have even experienced the unwelcoming nature of many Hungarians, where the government constructed a wire fence to keep refugees out of their territory. Put differently, it is hard to find the exact reasons why over one million Syrians and Iraqis chose to move to Germany rather than one of its neighbours.

This chapter analysed several possible reasons, highlighting that most asylum seekers were probably motivated by rational choice and tried to maximise their chances to 1) get a positive result on their asylum application, 2) to have a relatively comfortable life due to generous state support and good housing conditions, and 3) to integrate and find employment later. In many respects, Germany fared better than many other EU countries regarding the desirability among asylum seekers. This is not only because the German economy was doing well and its welfare system was more generous to asylum seekers than that of most other EU member states, but also because many asylum seekers had greater familiarity with Germany and knew people from their home country who had already settled there. Expecting both relatively strong support from the Germany government and population, but also from their own people in Germany, many refugees who fled Iraq and Syria after 2015 saw it as their best choice, and consequently tried to move there–in many cases, with success.

References

Altmeyer-Bartscher, M., Holtemöller, O., Lindner, A., Schmalzbauer, A., and Zeddies, G. (2016). On the distribution of refugees in the EU. *Intereconomics, 51* (4), 220–228

Berman, Y. (2018). *Falling on deaf ears. Asylum proceedings in Israel*. Retrieved from https://hotline.org.il/wp-content/uploads/2018/10/Eng-Web-RSD-Report-HRM-17Oct2018.pdf

Bertelsmann Stiftung (ed.) (2017). *Love it, leave it or change it? Junge Europäer in Mittel- und Osteuropa bekennen sich zur EU, sehen aber Notwendigkeit der Reformen.* Flashlight Europe Policy Brief 02/2017. Retrieved from https://www.bertelsmann-stiftung.de/fileadmin/files/BSt/Publikationen/GrauePublikationen/EZ_flashlight_europe_2017_02_DT.pdf

Bundeszentrale für politische Bildung (2020). *Asylbedingte Kosten und Ausgaben.* Retrieved from https://www.bpb.de/gesellschaft/migration/flucht/zahlen-zu-asyl/265776/kosten-und-ausgaben

Burmann, M. and Valeyatheepillay, M. (2017). Asylum recognition rates in the top 5 EU countries. *Ifo DICE Report, 2* (15), 48–50. Retrieved from https://www.ifo.de/DocDL/dice-report-2017-2-burmann-valeyatheepillay-june.pdf

Connor, P. (2018). *Most Syrians are in the Middle East, and about a million are in Europe.* Pew Research Center. Retrieved from https://www.pewresearch.org/fact-tank/2018/01/29/where-displaced-syrians-have-resettled/

Destatis (2016). *Asylbewerberleistungen: 169 % mehr Leistungsberechtigte im Jahr.* Pressemitteilung Nr. 304 vom 5. September 2016. Retrieved from https://www.destatis.de/DE/Presse/Pressemitteilungen/2016/09/PD16_304_222.html

Frykman, M. and Mäkelä, F. (2019). 'Only Volunteers'? Personal motivations and political ambiguities within the *Refugees Welcome to Malmö* civil initiative. In: Feischmidt, M., Pries, L., and Cantat, C. (eds.) *Refugee protection and civil society in Europe.* London: Palgrave Macmillan, 291–318

Hodali, D. and Prange, A. (2018). Asylum benefits in the EU: How member states compare. *Deutsche Welle, 19* June 2018. Retrieved from https://www.dw.com/en/asylum-benefits-in-the-eu-how-member-states-compare/a-44298599

Nye, C. (2018). Children 'attempting suicide' at Greek refugee camp. *BBC, 28* August 2018. Retrieved from https://www.bbc.com/news/world-europe-45271194

Poushter, J. (2016). *European opinions of the refugee crisis in 5 charts.* Pew Research Centre. Retrieved from https://www.pewresearch.org/fact-tank/2016/09/16/european-opinions-of-the-refugee-crisis-in-5-charts/

Reuters (2018). Japan took in 20 asylum seekers last year as nearly 20,000 applied. 13 February 2018. Retrieved from https://www.reuters.com/article/uk-japan-immigration-refugeesidUKKBN1FX12Q

Šabić, S. (2017). *The relocation of refugees in the European Union: Implementation of solidarity and fear.* Zagreb: Friedrich Ebert Foundation. Retrieved from https://library.fes.de/pdf-files/bueros/kroatien/13787.pdf

Sakellis, Y., Spyropopulpu, N. and Ziomas, D. (2016). *The refugee crisis in Greece in the aftermath of the 20 March 2016 EU-Turkey Agreement.* ESPN Flash Report, 2016/64. Retrieved from https://ec.europa.eu/social/BlobServlet?docId=16180&langId=en

United Nations High Commissioner for Refugees (UNHCR) (n.d.) *Convention and protocol relating to the status of refugees 1951 Convention 1967 Protocol.* Retrieved from https://www.unhcr.org/4ae57b489.pdf

ROMANIA:

IV

Looking for a better life abroad or in the city: why have so many Romanians left the countryside?

(Co-authored with Andrei HERINEAN)

Abstract   This chapter focuses on the outbound (internal & external) migration flow from rural areas in Romania, explaining the social, economic, political and demographic circumstances surrounding it. The general trend of urban transition visible in Romania in the last century (and its recent reversal), along with a certain amount of outward migration, is not unusual for a developing country. However, the Second World War and its geopolitical outcomes significantly impacted Romania's development. Decades of communist dictatorship followed by a less-than-ideal transition into democracy gave rise to an unstable political and economic climate, as well as considerable disparity between the richer and poorer regions and segments of the population. In this context, emigration has become a critical aspect of modern Romanian society, with millions of Romanians choosing to leave the country and move towards the West in search for employment and other opportunities. As a result, while the entire country is currently impacted, the comparatively poor rural parts of Romania suffer the gravest consequences.

What this chapter covers: Migration, internal migration, urban-rural divide, EU labour mobility, living conditions in Romania, modern history of Romania, poverty and social exclusion, rural depopulation

Introduction

When Romania joined the European Union in 2007, the country hoped that EU membership would translate into a significant development of infrastructure and raise the living standards. Particularly among the millions of rural dwellers, there were hopes that monetary support from the EU's regional development programs–as well as an increase in trade with EU nations–would lift many out of poverty. Although poverty has been declining over the previous 15 years, the living conditions of many rural dwellers are far from rosy: around three million live on less than US$ 5.50 a day, as employment opportunities are sparse. About half of the poorest 40% of Romanians–many of them living in rural areas–have no work, while another 28% live off subsistence agriculture, producing just enough food to support themselves.

Romania is one of the poorest and most unequal countries in the European Union. With nominal GDP per capita below US$13,000, national wealth is much lower than in all other EU member states apart from Bulgaria. The social groups most affected by poverty are rural inhabitants, the country's Roma minorities, and children. With 41.5% of children at risk of poverty or social exclusion in 2020, the prospects for many young Romanians are grim. In the countryside in particular, schooling is often substandard, with teachers and resources lacking. In fact, over one third of the countryside schools do not even have running water or flushable toilets.

With the number of farmers and small agricultural businesses declining, employment opportunities in rural areas are dwindling. This has led to an exodus from the countryside to urban and suburban areas over the past decades. Since Romania joined the EU in 2007, many people from Romania's more rural areas have also opted to start a new life in other EU member states, as EU membership brought about the possibility to move to and reside in any EU country (with all restrictions on their freedom of movement being lifted on January 1st, 2014). In fact, an estimated 3.6 million people–around 16% of the Romanian population–have left for foreign shores.

This chapter investigates the reasons why rural dwellers have left their villages in droves by analysing the socio-economic and political situation in the countryside. It reveals that the divide between urban and rural areas is much more pronounced than in most other EU member states, with rural dwellers often facing dismal living conditions, insufficient medical care, below-standard education, and a lack of employment opportunities. This has made millions of Romanians turn their backs on rural hometowns to move to more developed urban areas within Romania and abroad in search for employment, better opportunities, and a more comfortable life. Highlighting the sparse and fragmented provision of services for social protection, employment, education and healthcare in rural areas, this chapter argues that the bulk of migration away from the countryside is due to the socio-economic conditions that have improved only marginally, and at a much slower pace than in Romania's urban centres.

Rural development and poverty in Romania: the first half of the 20th century

For the longest part of its history, Romania had a rural, agriculture-based society. Larger cities, mostly built around natural fortresses and major trading hubs, certainly existed long before the country itself. However, even in the 1950s, almost 80% of the Romanian population resided in the rural areas, relying on small-scale subsistence agriculture, using nearly all their crops or livestock for personal consumption and not for sale or trade. While there were land reforms designed to decrease the overwhelming poverty, their success was insignificant, as their implementation was faulty and biased toward those in the middle and upper layers of society. As such, the overall living standards of the (poor) rural dwellers did not change to any meaningful extent.

During the first half of the 20th century, before the Communist Party declared the Romanian People's Republic in 1947, Romania was an agricultural society. In the interwar period (1918–1939) between WWI and WWII (the earliest time from which reliable statistics are available), around 80% of the Romanian population lived in the countryside, with agriculture as their main occupation. The majority led a life in poverty without any land possessions. According to the land ownership registries, up to the land reform in 1921, the richest 1% of landowners controlled around 52% of the working land, while the remaining of 99% of the people only held 48%. 600,000 Romanians owned no land whatsoever and had to rely on day labour and seasonal labour–working on the farms of richer landowners–to survive. Even those in the possession of land could often not make a living: at least two million families owned a piece of land too small to make ends meet, meaning they also had to work for other landowners or rely on income from other sources (Şandru, 1975: 23–26). For many villagers, the only source of income was their small plots of land, as they could sell or exchange some of the produce. In stark contrast, the richer landowners often had larger farms and massive tracts of land. As the affluent landowners lived in the city and rarely worked their own land, they either leased it to peasants in exchange for a yearly amount of produce, or hired workers. They also rarely managed their lands themselves, as this was commonly done via an intermediary–the *arendaş* (lessor)–who, in turn, imposed even higher rents on the poorer villagers. As a result, while landowners were largely unaffected by inflation and grain market prices, the peasants entered a vicious cycle of increasing their debt in order to survive. This made them unable to acquire land of their own, move to a better place, or receive any kind of education, keeping most of the rural population poor, uneducated and often in bad health (Eidelberg, 1974: 80-81). About half of the Romanian population in the interwar period could not read or write–a figure much higher than that of Japan, where already in the mid-Edo period, more than 50% of all men were literate.

Due to the lack of financial resources for most of the population and the high dependence on subsistence agriculture, Romania's economic development was far behind that of central European countries and Japan. Yavetz (1991: 599) describes this with the following words:

In 1918, Romania was a primitive country, where between 43 and 60 per cent of the population were illiterate, infant mortality ran at 17.4 per cent, and the annual per capita income was sixty dollars. Productivity was extremely low, industry at an embryonic stage, protective tariffs were very high, and most experts agree that 80 per cent of the population lived below the poverty line.

In other words, the living conditions of the average inhabitant were dire and the country much less advanced than the European average at that time.

The country's peasants had already revolted several times by this point, and in order to avoid further resurgence (as well as to reward the hundreds of thousands who had fought in the war, with more than 300,000 dead), the government finally implemented a long-proposed policy of distributing land to the poorer peasants. This 1921 Land Reform was based on massive expropriations, with the government taking all land above a certain threshold from the Crown and other institutions, wealthy landowners, and people residing outside Romania (among others). These landowners were reimbursed with long-term government bonds and their land was distributed to more than two million peasants, who had 20 years to pay for it (Sabates, 2005: 10). However, while this measure temporarily reduced the assets of the wealthiest, it failed to help the poor achieve comfortable living standards. Not only did it take an entire 16 years for the reform to be fully implemented but it also left the possessions of the middle-class landowners untouched. As a result, land distribution went from 1% of the population owning one half and 99% owning the other to about 10% owning half and 90% the other half. Moreover, the new landowners were often too poor to buy tools and animals to work the land, and since they had to pay for it nonetheless, most of them remained indebted. This condition continued all the way until the end of the Second World War (Şandru, 1975: 262–263).

Romania entered World War II on the Axis side, fighting together with Germany, Italy, and Japan. As a result, even though the country later changed sides and joined the Allies when the government was overthrown, Romania was treated as a German ally and loser at the end of the war. This meant it had to pay massive war reparations to the USSR ($11 billion in today's currency), lost a large amount of territory (such as the entire current Republic of Moldova), and ended up in the post-war Soviet sphere of influence. However, probably the most significant development was that, due to both internal unrest and pressure from the USSR, the Romanian Communist Party came to power.

A shift away from the countryside: Romania's industrialisation and urbanisation in the post-war years

The rise of the Romanian Communist Party (*PCR–Partidul Comunist Român*) in 1945 led to dramatic changes for the rural population. In an effort to catch up with other countries and to become more powerful, the new government implemented forced industrialisation, pushed for extensive (large-scale) agriculture oriented towards mass production, and developed Romania's infrastructure. The doctrine of the PCR included supporting labourers and reducing the income inequality; to achieve this they implemented another land reform in 1945. Unlike in 1921, the majority of landowners were forcefully expropriated, and this time they received no compensation; yet, those who received land still had to pay for it. The previous issues appeared once more, and living standards remained mostly the same for the poorer segments of the population, while the richer segments saw a significant decrease in wealth (Stoica, 2007: 288–290). As a result, despite reforms and a drive for industrialisation, most of Romania's rural population remained impoverished under the communist regime (1947–1989).

Moreover, it was not only the peasants that suffered. In 1948, one year after the Communist Party proclaimed Romania a republic (calling it the *People's Republic of Romania* first, and later the *Socialist Republic of Romania*) and installed a dictatorial regime, they nationalised the means of production, forcefully taking over all large and medium private enterprises in all fields of activity, as well as around 400,000 houses, restaurants, hotels, and other buildings (Stoica, 2007: 233–234). Many segments of society, such as entrepreneurs and businessmen, lost some of their wealth and most peasants–ranging from the wealthy peasants (known as *chiaburi*, also *kulak*s in Russian), the somewhat affluent ones and even the poorest farmers–were expropriated overnight, with no compensation, in 1949. The rural elites, such as teachers or priests, were threatened into becoming members of the new collective agricultural institutions (GACs). The collectivisation proceeded violently, with many people killed or severely injured during armed uprisings. At least 50,000 people were either imprisoned and sentenced to labour camps or directly deported to Romania's poor regions (Tismăneanu, 2006: 204). By the end of 1962, almost all the workable land in Romania was owned by the state and exploited by the GACs. This measure was supposed to increase productivity and general wealth by sharing agricultural equipment and buildings; however, the reality proved to be the opposite. Not only was productivity extremely low, but taxes were extremely high, with most of the money going toward paying Romania's war debt. Large parts of Romania's population remained impoverished and millions of people in rural areas continued to suffer from malnutrition well into the 1980s (Tismăneanu, 2006: 210–212). This lack of economic prosperity and development contributed to the system's collapse in 1989.

During the communist regime, a large exodus from the countryside to urban areas took place. While in 1956, 75% of all Romanians lived in rural regions, by 1985, a third of them had moved to urban areas, resulting in an equilibrium between the ratio of urban and rural dwellers. Ever since, more than half of the population (around 55% today) lives in urban areas. This massive exodus from the countryside to the cities was due to three main factors. The first was a combination of the country's failed collectivisation and rapid industrialisation. Farming no longer provided enough paid employment opportunities for people in the countryside, due in part to the government forcing students to work on farms for free during planting and harvesting seasons. As a result, many rural dwellers headed for cities, looking for jobs in the newly-opened factories (Stoica, 2007: 440). The following numbers impressively underline this phenomenon: while agriculture

Employment by sectors (in %), 1950–2017

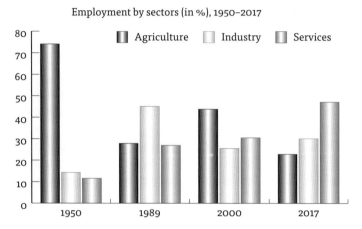

Fig. 4–1 Romanian employment according to sectors

(Andrei, 2018: 52)

employed three quarters of the workforce in 1950, the numbers changed drastically as the communist regime forced industrialisation, reaching 28% in 1989, while industry took up 45%.

> As agriculture became increasingly automated and lost importance as a part of the Romanian economy, the number of available jobs significantly decreased. This meant that the workforce had to either relocate or commute to a nearby city to find a job in one of the two other sectors.

The second factor was education: for the first time in Romanian history, education became truly universally available. In spite of the system's obvious shortcomings, which included strict ideological education, elimination of dissidents and harsh censorship, the government was successful in almost eradicating illiteracy throughout the entire population. While in 1930, the educational achievements of the rural population were dismal, with only around 25% of the population being able to read and write (out of which 90% had only attended primary school lasting two to four years), literacy increased to 94% by 1966 due to an intense education campaign that started in 1948 (Andrei, 2018: 72). Pursuing further education (in the cities) was encouraged by the state; however, as access to tertiary education was extremely competitive, many villagers had to move to urban centres to receive an education that allowed them to enter the state universities.

The third factor was the accelerated growth in population during the Communist regime. The government launched numerous policies geared towards population growth, resulting in Romania's resident population increasing by as much as 45% between 1945 and 1989, from a little over 16 million to 23 million in 1989. The reasons for this population explosion were manifold: First, Romania introduced forceful pro-natalist legislation, prohibiting abortion except for extreme cases. Second, it promoted large families and propagated the idea of "mother heroine", rewarding families with multiple children and punishing those with few or no children. Third, the regime strictly regulated international mobility, to the extent that nobody was allowed to leave the country except with approval from the government. This de-facto ban on leaving the country and the pro-natalist policies helped the government increase the population and, consequently, the country's labour force (Tismăneanu, 2006).

As the overall population increased at such high speed, life in the countryside became increasingly difficult because there was little work outside of farming and income from agricultural work was often not enough to support the growing families. Thus, large parts of the rural population moved to cities in search for better work and education opportunities, as well as for the chance of being assigned state housing.

This exodus to the cities is depicled in the graph below, which reveals the fast-paced growth of the urban population (as well as that of the overall population). While just over three million Romanians lived in urban areas in 1946, their number was close to 12 million in 1989, revealing a nearly four-fold increase in just over 40 years.

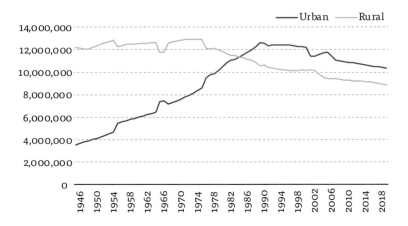

Fig. 4-2 Urban vs. rural population, 1946–2018

(Andrei, 2018: 28)

During the Communist regime from 1945 to 1989, most of the rural population remained poor despite several reforms, while urban dwellers' opportunities grew. As new workplaces and educational opportunities became available in the city, rural inhabitants migrated to urban areas at an unprecedented scale: within only three decades, one third of the population had moved to city areas hoping for a better life. As external migration (to foreign countries) was strictly controlled (and almost always forbidden) by the regime, the only way for many Romanians in the countryside to have a better life was to move to the urban areas in the country.

Moreover, among those still living in rural areas, many abandoned their agricultural activities and started commuting to the nearest city, working in the new factories and on construction sites. In the meantime, their children often pursued further education at a high school in the city.

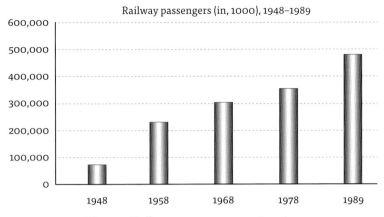

Fig. 4-3 Railway passengers, 1948–1989

(Based on Andrei, 2018: 286–287)

The infrastructure built between the 1950s and 1980s allowed hundreds of thousands of countryside residents to work or study in a nearby city, commuting by train. The popularity of such daily commutes from the countryside to the cities is revealed by the almost sevenfold increase in train passengers between 1948 and 1989.

Despite the growth in population and GDP, most of the rural population remained in poverty until the end of the Communist regime in 1989 (and beyond). When an economic recession hit the country in the 1980s, much of the country starved because the regime imposed strict austerity policies (so they could continue repaying Romania's war debt to the USSR). While most parts of the population were suffering, the large segment of the rural population who had lost their land during collectivisation was hit the hardest. Many of them moved to the cities for economic reasons or attempted to cross the border illegally, with thousands killed or injured (Duduciuc/Țiu,

2015)[1].

External migration: Romanians moving to European countries from the 1990s

Following Romania's economic crisis in the 1980s, which brought about a nationwide lack of basic necessities, the communist regime was overturned in 1989; as the country opened the borders once more, its citizens profited from the newly-found freedom and left in swathes. Most of them emigrated to central European countries such as France and Italy rather than searching for a new life in other eastern European countries. This was because most of Romania's eastern European neighbours were still suffering from the aftereffects of the URSS and offered fewer opportunities for a wealthy new life. African and Middle Eastern countries were also rather unattractive for Romanians looking for economic prosperity. As Romania has a Latin culture with a Latin-based language, Italy and France, with their Latin roots, became favourite destinations for many Romanian expats, as they felt a more intimate relationship with these countries than with Romania's closer (but mostly Slavic) neighbours Bulgaria, Ukraine and Hungary. Thus, in the early 1990s, the exodus towards western and southern Europe began.

Although the overturn of the communist regime brought about a liberalisation of the economy, the 1990s did not see any visible increase in standard of living. In fact, Romania's GDP declined right after the revolution, and remained lower than it was in the 1980s until the early 2000s. Although some state-owned enterprises were privatised and land confiscated during the collectivisation was returned to the previous owners (over the following ten years), millions of Romanians still lived in poverty. This is because, just like in the case of the previous land reforms, most of the land was split into very small pieces, making it just big enough for subsistence

---

[1] More than half of those involved in border incidents were low-level workers, farmers and unemployed people, accompanied by their families; intellectuals, who might have been fleeing for political or educational reasons, were only a small number.

agriculture. In addition, the new owners had neither the equipment nor the funds to cultivate it efficiently. As such, the rural regions, which at that point still relied almost entirely on agriculture for their economy, remained comparatively poor. The situation only deteriorated from 1992 onwards, when new austerity measures were implemented to counteract inflation (Roper, 2000: 82–97).

While countryside residents in the early 90s were suffering from poverty, their counterparts in the cities were not in a much better situation: de-industrialisation caused a massive loss of workplace, meaning many urbanites were without work and income. This led to an increase in internal migration in the 90s; however, unlike in previous decades, where people moved from rural to urban areas, the trend was reversed. Thousands of city dwellers that had moved to urban areas from the countryside returned to rural regions to start small-scale agriculture, a trend that continued until the early 2000s. However, as the service sector became the major player in the economy in the 2000s, more people began to agglomerate near cities, triggering the on-going suburbanisation phenomenon, with many people moving to the suburbs of Romania's major cities. Today, suburban centres are the only areas gaining population, while both remote rural areas and city centres suffer from negative demographical growth.

Why do tens of thousands of Romanians leave the countryside for (sub)urban areas or foreign countries year by year? What are their motivations and hopes when moving to the cities or abroad? In the following, we will analyse the current living conditions for large parts of the rural population.

Why do Romanians leave the countryside?

A plethora of reasons exist for why countryside dwellers choose to leave for either the cities or the West. Most of them stem from the drastic disparities in economic opportunity: while the capital, Bucharest, along with some other major cities, have reached and even surpassed the average per capita income in the EU, 70% of the rural population lives in poverty, showing that most of the country's wealth is concentrated in the urban areas. This disparity is more evident when we consider that 55% of all Romanians live in urban areas but around two thirds of the nearly five million poor citizens reside in the countryside, making poverty a distinctive feature of rural Romania (Habitat for Humanity, n.d.). Most of Romania's poor are farmers or unemployed rural workers, who have been trapped in poverty for decades without the capital needed to rise out of it. The massive infrastructure gap caused by the lack of investment and poor management severely limits the growth of rural areas, and the disconnection between central and local administration ensures that necessary funds often do not reach the more remote areas. In other words, while the EU (and to a lesser extent, also the Romanian government) has tried to raise the living standards in rural areas, many of the policies did not result in success.

What is life in the countryside like? Let us look at the living conditions many rural inhabitants face in Romania. Poverty is still a dominant feature of the Romanian countryside. While it has been declining, nearly a quarter of Romanians (4.6 million people, about three million being rural dwellers) live on less than $5.50 a day. This share is considerably higher than in any other EU country. Many poor rural inhabitants have no work: if we look at the poorest 40% of Romanians, we can see that half of them do not work, with another 28% living off subsistence agriculture (De Rosa/Kim, 2018). Poverty is often inherited, with 1.5 million children being born into poverty. This makes Romania the country with the highest rate of children at risk of poverty or social exclusion in the EU, standing at 41.5% in 2020.

While among Bucharest's population, around 95% are considered 'not poor', a World Bank (2017) report found that only 72% of rural dwellers are 'not poor', while 28% are below the poverty line. Poverty appears to be rampant, especially among the young and the uneducated: child poverty of Romanians under 14 years is as high as 28%, and among those over 16 without education, poverty reaches a whopping 47%. Among the Roma (a Romanian minority group of around 1.85 million), poverty rates are as high as 77%–also because less than one third of adult Roma ethnics are in employment, while only 36% of those aged 16-24 are studying or working, with the numbers about one third lower for women (Gazibar/Giuglea, 2019 & European Union Agency for Fundamental Rights, 2018).

The living conditions in the countryside are often dismal, and much below what people would expect from an EU member state. Basic necessities, such as access to potable water, are often not met for millions of rural dwellers. According to World Bank figures, about 20% of people in the countryside (equalling just under two million people) do not have water safe for drinking or for cooking at home. Habitat for Humanity (n.d.) even suggests that as many as 41% of Romanians have no access to running water at home, while the World Bank (2017) finds that a third of rural households lack a flushing toilet, which unsurprisingly results in unsanitary living conditions. This is not only true for households; institutional buildings suffer from the same issue: 38% of schools in rural areas have no indoor toilets or access to clean drinking water–a figure 5.5 times higher than that of schools in cities, where only 7% are in this situation. In particular, villages in Romania's North-East development region, which is among the five poorest in the EU, suffer from these issues.

The lack of adequate housing is another big factor for the exodus of Romanians. The EAN's (2020) *Poverty Watch 2020: Romania* report estimates that around 30% of Romanian households are based in improper dwellings or slums, often facing forced eviction because their homes are built without permission. Those who do have proper housing often live in old apartments, in one of the 10,000 blocks of flats built by the Communists that have fallen into disrepair–one third of Romanian housing, in fact, is in urgent need of rehabilitation. Many homes are also crowded; it is not uncommon for both urban and rural families to share a single room among four and more family members, which makes life stressful and potentially unhygienic. According to Habitat for Humanity (n.d.), a "family of eight is typically more likely to live in a two-room flat than in a house". In other words, many Romanians live in low-quality accommodation that is insufficient in size, often without proper heating and running water, under conditions that endanger the residents' health. Moreover, the severe floods that occurred over the past years have left thousands of rural Romanians in temporary shelters. Due to the country's harsh winter with heavy snowfall, especially in its eastern areas, many villagers are cut off for days or weeks, as the snow blocks the main roads and limits stable food supplies (Housing for Habitat, n.d.).

The reasons for such high poverty rates in the countryside stem, to a large extent, from the low educational attainments of Romania's population. Not only does Romania have the lowest rate of people with tertiary education in the EU (just over 25%), but many Romanians do not even complete basic education. 15% of all kids (three quarters of them Roma ethnics) abandoned school without any diploma in 2020, 5% more than the EU average, while in the countryside school dropout rates go as high as 26% (Statista, 2022). Furthermore, although 96% of the population has learned to read and write, functional illiteracy is still high. A whopping 40% of Romania's students are believed to be unable to apply their basic reading and writing skills to real-life circumstances. While they can technically read or write, they often cannot make sense of newspapers, understand contracts, or do basic calculations when shopping (De Rosa/Kim, 2018).

> School dropout rates have improved overall since 2011 but remain consistently at 5% or more above the EU average.

A major factor for the low educational attainments of Romanian youngsters is low government spending. Education expenditure in Romania is among the lowest in the EU, standing at only 3.6% of GDP in 2019. This is 1.1% points lower than the EU average of 4.7%, and around half that of top-spending countries such as Sweden (6.9%) (Eurostat, 2019a). The lack of sufficient financing for education in Romania translates directly into an insufficient number of schools. As a result, 56% of students are in overcrowded schools, according to the country's Ministry of Education (Romania Insider, 2017).

It is not surprising that, the countryside suffers from a lack of adequate learning facilities in regard to the number of schools, the student-teacher ratio, and equipment. While 45% of the students below high school level live in the countryside, only 35% of teachers

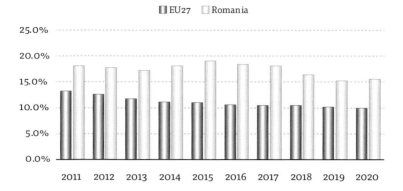

Fig. 4–4 School dropout rates, Romania vs. EU average

(Statista, 2022)

work there. This means that the student-teacher ratio is unfavourable in rural areas, making it harder for students to progress. Those countryside students who still manage to learn enough to pursue high school education generally need to relocate to urban areas, as only 8% of high schools are located in the countryside. In other words, from the beginning, students in rural areas face fewer educational chances than their peers in the city, and attending high school often comes with the burden of long commutes to urban areas or even relocation. As such commutes or moves cost money, a fair share of students in the countryside leave school early, not finishing the compulsory ten years of education for economic reasons. This has led to the rate of school dropouts in the countryside being at least twice as high as in the rest of the country (Iagăr, 2021).

Another reason for the low educational achievement is the lack of focus on schooling among the Roma minority. To begin with, 78% of Roma ethnics are at or below the poverty line, and 84% of their households have no sanitary facilities or electricity; more than half of Roma citizens do not participate in any remunerated activity, and only a third of their children even attend kindergarten. This situation is due to centuries of social exclusion, which now translate into ghettoisation and rejection on both the Romanian majority and the Roma minority side. Projects aimed at the education, rehabilitation and integration of Roma ethnics are slow and fragmented, and the coordination between the central and local authorities is lacking, as it appears that the Roma are far from being a priority (Gazibar/ Giuglea, 2019).

The failure of state institutions is not only evident in education: the medical sector, for example, is severely underfunded, and especially in the countryside, access to hospitals and (trustworthy) doctors is difficult. The following figures reveal the vast gap in medical access between urban and city dwellers: out of the 650 hospitals and inpatient clinics, only 8% are in the rural areas. Access to regular GPs can be difficult, as only 40% of them practise in the countryside (Andrei, 2019: 46–47). Even if physicians are located nearby, it is often hard to get appointments, as countryside GPs tend to have 50% more registered patients than family physicians in the city, the Romanian Ombudsman reports. The proportion for other medical professions (non-GP) is even higher: a medical specialist has, on average, eight times more patients than their colleagues in the city, a dentist six times, and a pharmacist four times (Avocatul Poporului, 2021: 3). This greatly highlights the inequality between the city and the countryside regarding access to the country's medical system.

Why are there so few doctors in the countryside? For many of the well-educated professions, who received their education (and often also their training) in the cities, working in the countryside is not attractive. Not only are wages lower and living conditions often worse, but the job is often also more difficult and time-consuming. As mentioned before, countryside medics need to attend to more patients, which translates into longer working hours. In addition, while the average family physician in an urban environment has their entire patient base within a comparatively close distance, those working in the rural areas are often assigned entire communes comprised of several villages. In practice, a 1.5 times higher patient base involves commuting upward of 100 kilometres every day, often on roads fallen into disrepair.

Due to the underfunding of the medical system, the inequality of access to doctors in the countryside and the city, and the lack of hospitals and specialised physicians in many remote areas, medical

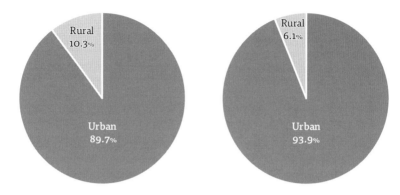

State-owned hospitals with inpatient care   Private hospitals with impatient care

Fig. 4–5 Hospitals and clinics with inpatient care, rural vs. urban

(Andrei, 2019: 46)

care in rural Romania remains insufficient and rarely rises above the most basic level. This means many countryside residents fail to receive the medical care they would need, especially among the elderly, which shortens their (healthy) life expectancy and further widens the gap between the city and rural areas.

Another reason why life in the Romanian countryside can be hard is the lack of sufficient employment opportunities. In Q1 2020, the labour force participation rate for people aged 15-64 reached 68.4%; although this shows consistent improvement, it did not reach the 70% target set by the Romanian government and the EU, according to a report by the National Institute of Statistics (INSSE, 2021). Moreover, Trading Economics (n.d.) statistics show that Romania's labour force participation rate of 64.8% in Q1 2021 was much lower than the EU average (73.3%), and while the numbers recovered somewhat by Q3 2021, they are still 8.5% below the EU average.

Although employment rates are below EU average, Romania has some of the lowest rates of unemployment in the EU, standing at an average of 4.84% in 2020–a figure comparable to countries like Germany, though the COVID crisis brought the unemployment rate to a peak 5.7% in April 2021 (World Bank, 2022; Statista, 2022b & Statista, 2022a). This brings up to the following question: Considesing the country's low unemployment rates, why are less than two thirds of the working-age population in employment?

There are several reasons why more than 30% of working-age Romanians are either unemployed or not part of the active workforce at all. A primary factor is the comparatively low labour force participation rate of women. A World Bank statistic shows that 41.9% of women aged 15-64 were not part of the labour force in 2019 while that was the case for only 21.8% of men in the same age group (World Bank, 2021a and 2021b). This is predominantly due to entrenched gender norms and the lack of part-time employment. Since women are considered responsible for raising children and caring for elderly parents and in-laws, they are often trapped in unpaid household and care work. Relatively generous maternity benefits also keep many women, who had worked before childbirth, out of the labour market. This lack of employment, as well as the unwillingness of some women to work, leads to higher rates of poverty among women than men, especially in old age.

Romania has the highest pension gap in all EU member states, with women receiving around 60% fewer pensions than men because of their lower pay and shorter employment. This contributes to many Romanian women being at risk of poverty and social exclusion at old age (European Commission, 2017a). Pension coverage is much lower in the countryside than in the cities (as many farmers have not paid into the social security system), and the trend is negative. As social spending in Romania is among the lowest in the EU, standing at only 14.4% of GDP (about half that of many other member states), pensions are far from generous: although they have been on the rise in recent years, almost doubling since 2015, the average pension in 2020 was only 1,500 lei, or €300 (Statista, 2022d). At the same time, the proportion of rural inhabitants eligible for a pension is decreasing, which means that, overall, less funding is directed toward the countryside, with visible negative effects on the local economy.

Another reason for the low labour force participation in Romania is the relatively high number of people engaged in subsistence agriculture in the countryside. As they are not employed or not registered as self-employed, they do not show up in the official statistics. The lack of larger lands, appropriate tools and machinery, however, means that it is impossible for these peasants to yield considerable income from their land and the produce they sell. A World Bank (2018) report shows that the average output per hectare of land cultivated is only 42% of the EU average, while the average output per worker is a meagre 22%. In concrete numbers, a hectare of land in Romania was used to cultivate only €818 worth of produce in one year while it was €2,400 in Italy. Similarly, a Romanian agricultural worker only accounted for €7,722 of produce–around 15% of the almost €50,000 in Italy.

A result of the low level of education, low employment, the underutilisation of labour and high rates of poverty is that the gap between the Romanian rich and the poor is the highest in the EU. The Gini Index of equivalised disposable income stood at 34.8% in 2018, making it the third highest in the EU and considerably higher than the EU average of 30.2% (Eurostat, 2022). The inequality level of Romania was over 7.0; in other words, the top 20% had over seven times more than the bottom 20%. In the rest of the EU, it was around 5.1. What is more, inequality has been on the rise since 2018 due to high inequality of market incomes (EU Commission, 2020). The deepening gap between the rich and the poor stems from the rising income for the country's top earners, while those with a low salary often saw their income decrease. In fact, the poorest 40% of Romanians have experienced one of the greatest declines of income shares in the EU. As Romania is not a welfare state, income remains largely in the hands of the wealthy, and the redistributive effect of the tax and benefit system is marginal. As a result, the more disadvantaged parts of Romanian society are mostly left out. The Poverty Watch 2020 report describes this social problem with the following words: "Inequality of opportunities remains one of the main challenges for Romania: unequal access to education, healthcare and other services, along with intergenerational transmission of poverty, prevents children or families from disadvantaged areas from reaching their full potential" (EAPN, 2020).

To summarise, while Romania's poverty rate has slightly decreased in the recent years, the Romanian countryside is still plagued by monetary poverty. An SDG Watch report shows that Romania's population at risk of poverty or social exclusion is more than 70% higher than the EU average, with the rural population being affected at more than twice the rate of the urban population (Gazibar/Giuglea, 2019). Low education contributes to this, as only 46% of those who left school without completing compulsory education were part of the workforce in 2019. Particularly affected by this are the Roma ethnics, who, in spite of the recent inclusionary policies and educational programs, still make up three quarters of the early school abandonment cases. Comparatively, Romanian cities fare much better. School abandonment rates are in the single digits and poverty rates are below 15%, and the trend appears to be positive. This, coupled with the visible disparity in terms of health services and work opportunities, has made many rural dwellers try to escape their dire situation by moving to Romania's urban and suburban areas or abroad, as their situation is unlikely to improve in the countryside.

> While poverty rate has slightly decreased in recent years, the Romanian countryside is still plagued by monetary poverty. An SDG Watch report shows that Romania has a population at risk of poverty or social exclusion more than 70% higher than the EU. average, with the rural population being affected at more than twice the rate of the urban population.

Infrastructure

Infrastructure deficiencies further complicate the situation. In 2017, Romania was ranked 103rd out of 137 countries in terms of overall infrastructure, with roads ranked at an abysmal 120 (World Economic Forum, 2017: 247). The current Romanian transport infrastructure,

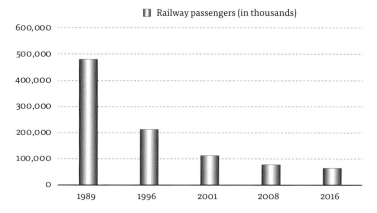

Fig. 4–6 Railway passengers, 1989–2016

(based on Andrei, 2018: 286–287)

in particular the railroads, was mostly built before 1989, and has had few upgrades ever since. The total length of usable train lines actually decreased by almost 500 kilometres between 1989 and 2006, while the number of available locomotives and carriages dropped by almost 30%. As trains were (and still are) the most common and affordable means of transportation for rural inhabitants, this translated into commuting becoming increasingly difficult for both students and workers. As of 2018, the number of railway passengers has fallen 7.5 times compared to 1989 and has even dropped below pre-WW2 figures (Andrei, 2018: 286–287). Moreover, the circulation of goods is severely impeded due to the subpar quality of both the roads and the rail lines. As a result, rural areas are still trailing behind urban ones in terms of overall economic opportunities.

> After the fall of the Communist regime, the number of railway passengers returned to pre-WWII levels within less than 30 years.

One of the main factors that delays the economic development of rural regions is the relative disconnection between central and

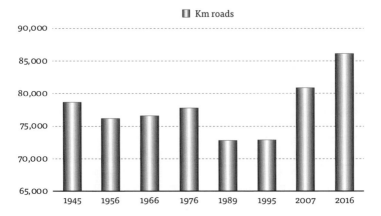

Fig. 4-7 Length of paved roads, 1945–2016

(based on Andrei, 2018: 268–69)

local authorities, which inevitably leads to misguided policies and underutilisation of the labour force available in rural regions. The Romanian government received significant sums prior to EU accession from the rural development program SAPARD to support the rural population, including initiatives to repair and upgrade the transport infrastructure. After joining the EU in 2007, Romania has continued to receive billions of euros in funding: between 2014 and 2020 alone, 4.6 billion euro were allocated for improving the transport and energy infrastructure (European Commission, n.d.b) However, not only is the overall absorption of EU funds one of the lowest in the entire EU, at only 56% overall, but the money received is also visibly underutilised (European Commission, n.d.a). In 2020, the country still had over 9,000 km of non-paved roads and 18,000 km of gravel roads, mostly located in rural areas, which represented almost one third of the road infrastructure available (Botea, 2020). High-rank roads face the same issue: only around 620 km of highway were built between 2007 and 2021, averaging 44 km per year, one of the slowest construction rates in the EU. This has resulted in a major impact on road freight transport, both at a national and international level.

> Only 14,000 km of new paved roads were built or upgraded between 1989 and 2016, of which only 747 kilometers were highways.

Foreign migration

Romania's accession to the EU in 2007 came with the right to free movement and the gradual opening of the EU labour market for Romanians, allowing its citizens to migrate towards richer Western countries (e.g. Germany, the UK, Spain, Italy, France) to achieve economic, professional, or educational fulfilment. As a result, an unprecedented number of Romanians left the country, rushing to fill the labour market gaps elsewhere. Although the global financial crisis of 2008-10 temporarily slowed down the pace of emigration, hundreds of thousands of Romanians leave their country year by year. Moreover, while the primary drive for early emigration was finding any employment, many of the recent emigrants are skilled or highly-skilled professionals who hope to advance their career abroad or who are searching for a better political system and more social and personal freedom. Considering that Romania ranks 126 out of 137 countries in terms of the government ensuring policy stability, and 113/137 in long-term vision of the authorities, it comes as no surprise that not only poorer residents, but also people looking for a stable environment are prone to emigration (World Bank, 2019: 478).

Due to the rapid changes in migration flows within the EU, it is impossible to find out the exact number of Romanian emigrants. However, by compiling data from population censuses in various countries, existing estimates place the Romanian diaspora (as of 2019) at around 4.4 million people, not including children born abroad. Even today, a significant percentage of the country's population considers emigrating. Among those, more than half want to leave the country for purely economic reasons, while others look for educational opportunities, better career options, and a more

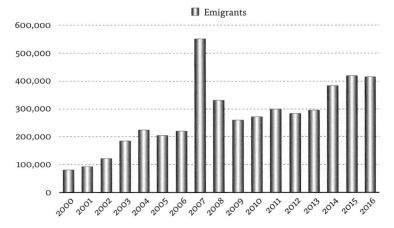

Fig. 4-8 Migration flow of Romanian citizens to OECD countries, 2000–2016

(OECD, 2018: 52)

favourable social environment. As a result, Romania's net migration remains negative, with over 50,000 more people moving out of Romania than into the country every year since 2013.

The graph below visualises the migration flow of Romanian citizens to OECD (mainly EU) countries, showing that emigration peaked in 2007, when Romania joined the European Union, and has been growing steadily since 2009.

If in the early 1990s, most migrants headed towards Germany, the US and Israel, later trends visibly favoured Italy, Spain, and the United Kingdom. What most external migrants have in common, though, is that they moved to an OECD country, resulting in 95% of all Romanian emigrants residing in just ten OECD countries in 2016. OECD and World Bank reports show that in the 1980s and early 90s, economic assistance from the host countries played a key role in emigration, which is why Germany, Hungary and Israel (which offered funding for German, Hungarian and Jewish ethnics) were initially the top destinations. As the emigration patterns diversified, improved relationships between Romania and southern European countries allowed small Romanian communities to form in countries like Italy and Spain, as well as the UK to the north-west.

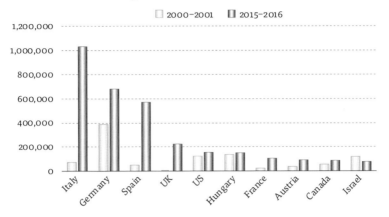

Fig. 4-9 Main destination countries for Romanian
emigrants aged 15 and above

(OECD, 2018: Table 1.1)

In turn, material and moral support from these already-established communities allowed more and more Romanians to establish lives for themselves, creating a positive reinforcement cycle. Cultural and linguistic barriers appear to play a role as well, with the current top choices being similarly Latin countries (e.g. Italy and Spain) as well as Germany, a country that already had a Romanian minority before 2007 (OECD, 2018; World Bank, 2018).

A notable outcome of west-bound emigration is the amount of remittances sent back to Romania. While in 1997, the amount of money received by the emigrants' families was around €456 million, it had already reached €8.5 billion, or as much as 5.5% of Romania's GDP, in 2008. Although remittances decreased significantly during the European financial and sovereign debt crisis, they once again increased rapidly after 2017 (Hórvath, 2009: 396; OECD, 2018: 32). Many impoverished rural communities have benefitted significantly from these remittances, as the largest share appears to be used to increase the overall living standards in rural households. This can be seen from macro-economic indicators, such as rural household consumption increasing considerably faster than GDP growth. Substantial amounts go into real estate for purchasing, constructing, or renovating houses, and a large share also goes into cars and consumer electronics. The ill effect of such spending is that the households (and on a larger scale, localities with high emigration rates) become economically dependent on remittances (Hórvath, 2009: 399–400). But it is not only rural areas that benefit: at already more than 5% of Romania's GDP in 2008, the money Romanian workers consistently send home forms a not insignificant share of the entire Romanian economy, leading to GDP growth and higher living standards across the country.

Emigration of Romanian citizens has several advantages, but also considerable disadvantages for Romanian society. Their remittances to left-behind family members increase consumption, which contributes to economic growth and provides poor rural families with the financial means to improve their living standards, including their housing situation, and to invest in education. Those emigrants who return to Romania often bring considerable capital accumulated overseas and new skills and connections, which they can use to improve the Romanian labour market and economy. Several emigrants who move back to Romania have used their experience and skills for entrepreneurial activities, founding companies and employing local people. Having unemployed workers move abroad also lessens the burden on the social systems; moreover, and, having been part of the labour force abroad makes them more employable upon their return to Romania.

However, many Romanian migrants have little desire to return to their home country, keeping net migration in the negative, a figure that has consistently increased since 1990 (Eurostat, 2019b). Today, 30% of the available workforce resides outside the country's borders, and immigration to Romania from both nationals and non-nationals remains low. As a result, Romanian agriculture is dwindling, the industrial sector is stagnating or declining, and the tertiary sector suffers from a severe lack of manpower. While the cities expand in territory as the suburban areas continue to develop, the isolated rural areas are left primarily with the elderly, who cannot or will not move away. As they eventually pass away, their villages will be completely deserted.

Additionally, the high number of emigrants and the hundreds of thousands of children who grow up without at least one parent takes its toll on the Romanian society. Many economic emigrants leave their children in Romania under the care of either the other parent (unless both parents leave, which is increasingly common) or grandparents (most commonly), as well as other members of the extended family. Within the relatively conservative and traditionalist Romanian society, this represents a serious threat to the idea of the traditional family. While in the 1990s, the male partner would often emigrate first, leaving the mother to take care of the children, the share of women emigrating has increased significantly over the past 15 years. In the 2006/7 school year, there were 170,000 Romanian school children with at least one parent abroad, out of which 35,000 had both parents away (Hórvath, 2009: 401). Even though the direct financial outcomes are usually positive, with children of emigrants having higher living standards on average, the number of dysfunctional households is on the increase, and children in this category are considered high-risk for psychological issues such as depression (Gazibar/Giuglea, 2019).

In the future, all these issues are prone to increase, as migration flows do not seem likely to change any time soon. Among Romanians aged 15 to 24 years interviewed in 2009 and 2018, almost 50% intended to emigrate and many had concrete plans for the following 12 months (OECD, 2018: Fig. 2.8).

This has a severe impact on population ageing, labour shortages, rural decline, and population growth. Combining the high emigration figures with the negative natural growth (Romania's fertility rate, at 1.76 children per woman in 2019, is far below the replacement level of 2.1), predictions for the overall Romanian population are grim. If current trends continue, the Romanian population will decrease by 9%, reaching 17 million in 2050; what is even more concerning is that rural areas are predicted to lose up to 25% of their population. By 2070, the overall population is expected to drop by more than 30%, while the rural population will decrease by around 50% compared to 2019. Similarly, the country's median age, currently at 43, will reach 50 by 2050, and the population over 65 will increase to 30%, which means that fewer people in the workforce will have to support the growing number of elderly people (Eurostat 2019b, 2020). This makes Romania's high emigration and low fertility rates a demographic time bomb.

This situation is unlikely to improve substantially in the near future. Reports by Eurostat, OECD, and the World Bank show that the current migratory trends are not likely to be reversed, leading to a decrease in overall population of another four million by 2070, as well as the abandonment of many rural settlements.

In the beginning, emigration was undoubtedly a positive thing for Romania, as migrants would send much of their income to their families back in Romania. However, as time passed, the sheer amount of people that left impacted the available national workforce. Current statistics show that Romani's working population is not sufficiently big to economically support its retirees, and migration flows do not appear to be changing directions.

The provision of social services for social protection, employment, education, and healthcare is fragmented and sparse, especially in rural areas where the needs (and the economic benefits) are greatest.

Conclusion

Over the past hundred years, Romanian society has evolved significantly and in abrupt leaps. From a predominantly agrarian country with an overwhelmingly poor population up until the early 1940s, Romania was forcefully propelled into the lines of developing countries, with the communist regime imposing draconian measures in order to repay external debt, develop the industry and infrastructure, and bring up literacy rates. For all that, as the regime somewhat revitalised the country itself, it also caused the death of millions, whether through direct oppression or because of the deficient policies that led to nationwide famine. This resulted in a second major step in 1989, when a new regime offered the people what they never had during communism: freedom of movement, trade and speech. What the new democratic regime did not offer people, though, was freedom from corruption–but the European Union offered support in that direction. In order to become a part of the EU, Romania was forced (and helped) to bring agriculture, infrastructure and education up to par, and also had to convince the EU Commission that the fight against corruption was a national priority. The endeavour proved successful, and in 2007, Romania joined the European Union. A virtual lack of country borders for Romanians has been guaranteed ever since, as has socio-economic assistance from the Union.

In spite of all this, Romania is still struggling. One hundred years ago, the top 1% of the population was wealthier than the bottom 99% combined. Today, the top 20% of the population still owns seven times as much as the bottom 20%. Rural areas still have one single medic covering ten remote villages, more students per teacher and less-equipped schools than cities, poor infrastructure with decrepit roads and one train every few hours. This is the result of rapid growth with an unstable foundation under a consistently corrupt regime. The only hope, for many, can be found across the border, and thus people leave the country by the millions. In particular, the countryside has experienced a huge population decline over the past decades, as both employment opportunities and family were declining.

High emigration rates of Romanians have brought numerous benefits for the country, such as considerable remittances for the families staying behind, which increased their quality of life and helped rural areas to develop, as well as new skills, connections and capital brought back to Romania by those emigrants who returned. However, it has also severely impacted the labour market, leading to labour shortages (also in vital professions such as medical services) and a failing pension system, as well as the greying of society and the dying of many rural villages.

References

Andrei, T. (ed.) (2018). *România: un secol de istorie–date statistice* [Romania: one century of history–statistical data]. Buchaest: Editura Institutului Național de Statistică

Ibid. (ed.) (2019). *România în cifre–breviar statistic* [Romania in numbers–statistical briefing]. Bucharest: Editura Institutului Național de Statistică

Avocatul Poporului (2021). *Raport special privind lipsa medicilor de familie din zona rurală și din zonele defavorizate sau greu accesibile* [Special report regarding the scarcity of family physicians in the rural area and from impoverished or isolated areas]. Bucharest: Romanian Ombudsman

Axenciuc, V, and Georgescu, G. (2018). *Gross domestic product–national income of Romania 1862–2010. Secular statistical series and methodological foundations.* MPRA Paper No. 84614. Retrieved from https://mpra.ub.uni-muenchen.de/84614/1/MPRA_paper_84614.pdf

Botea, R. (2020). Situația la zi a infrastructurii rutiere din România. *Ziarul Financiar*, 11 November 2020. Retrieved from https://www.zf.ro/zf-transporturi/situatia-zi-infrastructurii-rutiere-romania-889-km-autostrada-dintre-19738443

Comprehensive Census of the Romanian Population. 1930. Retrieved from https://ia801600.us.archive.org/1/items/recensamntulgeneo2inst/recensamntulgeneo2inst.pdf

Commission of the European Communities (2004). *2004 Regular report on Romania's progress towards accession.* COM (2004) 657. Retrieved from https://web.archive.org/web/20060425070733/http://europa.eu.int/comm/enlargement/report_2004/pdf/rr_ro_2004_en.pdf

Craciunoiu, C., Axworthy, M., and Scafes, C. (1995). *Third axis fourth ally: Romanian armed forces in the European war, 1941–1945.* London: Arms & Armour

Duduciuc, A., and Țiu, I. (2015). *Escape from communism. Last Romanians' migration waves during '80s.* Proceedings of the International Conference Education and Creativity for a Knowledge-based Society, Edition IX: 37–42

Eidelberg, P. (1974). *The Great Romanian Peasant Revolt of 1907: Origins of a modern jacquerie.* Leiden: Brill

European Anti-Poverty Network (2020). *Poverty Watch 2020: Romania.* Retrieved from https://www.eapn.eu/wp-content/uploads/2020/10/EAPN-EAPN-Romania-Poverty-Watch-2020_ENG-4707.pdf

European Commission (n.d.a) *2014–2020 ESIF overview.* Retrieved from https://cohesiondata.ec.europa.eu/overview

European Commission (2020). *Country report Romania 2020.* Retrieved from https://eur-lex.europa.eu/legal-content/EN/TXT/?uri=CELEX:52020SC0522

European Commission (2017a). *European semester thematic factsheet: Women in the labour market.* Retrieved from https://ec.europa.eu/info/sites/default/files/european-semester_thematic-factsheet_labour-force-participation-women_en_0.pdf

European Commission (n.d.b). *Large infrastructure operational programme: Romania.* Retrieved from https://ec.europa.eu/regional_policy/en/atlas/programmes/2014-2020/

romania/2014r016m10p001#:~:

European Commission (2017b). *Report from the Commission to the European Parliament and the Council. On progress in Romania under the Cooperation and Verification Mechanism.* Retrieved from
https://ec.europa.eu/info/files/progress-report-romania-2017-com-2017-44_en

European Commission (2019). *Report from the Commission to the European Parliament and the Council. On Progress in Romania under the Cooperation and Verification Mechanism.* COM (2019) 499. Retrieved from
https://ec.europa.eu/info/sites/default/files/progress-report-romania-2019-com-2019-499_en.pdf

European Union Agency for Fundamental Rights (2018). *Transition from education to employment of young Roma in nine EU Member States.* Luxembourg: Publications Office of the European Union. Retrieved from
https://fra.europa.eu/sites/default/files/fra_uploads/fra-2018-eu-midis-ii-roma-transition-education-employment_en.pdf

Eurostat (2019a). *Government expenditure on education.* Retrieved from
https://ec.europa.eu/eurostat/statistics-explained/index.php?title=Government_expenditure_on_education#Large_differences_between_countries_in_the_importance_of_expenditure_on_education

Eurostat. 2019b. *Population and demography statistics.* Retrieved from
https://ec.europa.eu/eurostat/web/population-demography

Eurostat (2020). *Demographic changes in Europe–national files: Romania.* Retrieved from
https://ec.europa.eu/eurostat/documents/10186/10990320/RO-RO.pdf

Eurostat (2022). *Gini coefficient of equivalised disposable income–EU-SILC survey.* Retrieved from
https://appsso.eurostat.ec.europa.eu/nui/show.do?dataset=ilc_di12

Gazibar, M. and Giuglea, L. (2019). *Inequalities in Romania: Despite recent improvements in Romania, poverty and income inequality remain high, and regional disparities are deepening.* SDG Watch Europe. Retrieved from
https://www.sdgwatcheurope.org/wp-content/uploads/2019/06/13.3.a-report-RO.pdf

Habitat for Humanity (n.d.) *Housing poverty in Romania.* Retrieved from
https://www.habitatforhumanity.org.uk/country/romania/

Hitchins, K. (1994). *The Oxford history of Modern Europe. Romania 1866-1947.* New York: Oxford University Press

Hórvath, I. and Anghel, G. (2009). Migration and its consequences for Romania. *Südosteuropa, 57* (4), 386–403

Iagăr, E. (ed.) (2021). *Sistemul educaţional în România–Date sintetice* [Educational system in Romania–synthetic data]. Bucharest: Editura Institutului Naţional de Statistică

INSSE (2021). *Labor force occupation rate and unemployment.* Retrieved from
https://insse.ro/cms/sites/default/files/com_presa/com_pdf/somaj_2020r.pdf

Marinescu, I. (2021). Increasing the accessibility of the population in rural and isolated areas to primary healthcare. *Romanian Journal of Information Technology and Automatic Control, 31* (2), 69–82

OECD (2019). *Talent abroad: A review of Romanian emigrants.* Paris: OECD Publishing. Retrievedfrom https://www.oecd-ilibrary.org/employment/talent-abroad-a-review-of-romanian-emigrants_bac53150-en

OECD Health Statistics (2020). *Health expenditure in relation to GDP*. Retrieved from https://www.oecd-ilibrary.org/sites/860615c9-en/index.html?itemId=/content/component/860615c9-en

Reuters (2018). *Anti-government protest in Romania turns violent*. Retrieved from https://www.reuters.com/article/us-romania-protests/anti-government-protest-in-romania-turns-violent-idUSKBN1KV1YO

Romania Insider (2017). Ministry: A third of Romanian schools do not have indoor toilets. *Romania Insider*, 7 November 2017. Retrieved from https://www.romania-insider.com/romanian-schools-indoor-toilets/

Roper, S. (2000). *Romania: The unfinished evolution*. Singapore: Harwood Academic Publishers

Sabates, R. (2005). *Cooperation in the Romanian countryside: An Insight into post-soviet agriculture*. New York: Lexington Books

Șandru, D. (1975). *Reforma agrară din 1921 în România* [1921 land reform in Romania]. Bucharest: Editura Academiei Republicii Socialiste România

Statista (2022a). *Impact of the coronavirus (COVID-19) outbreak on the labor market indicators in Romania from February 2020 to May 2021*. Retrieved from https://www.statista.com/statistics/1119871/romania-labor-market-indicators/

Statista (2022b). *Germany: Unemployment rate from 1999 to 2020*. Retrieved from https://www.statista.com/statistics/375209/unemployment-rate-in-germany/

Statista (2022c). *School dropout rate in Romania from 2011 to 2020*. Retrieved from https://www.statista.com/statistics/1103336/school-dropout-rate-romania/

Statista (2022d). *Average monthly pension in Romania from 2015 to 2020 (in Romanian lei)*. Retrieved from https://www.statista.com/statistics/1128078/romania-average-monthly-pension/

Stoica, S. (ed.) (2007). *Dicționar de istorie a Românie* [Dictionary of Romanian history]. Bucharest: Editura Merona

Tismăneanu, V. (ed.) (2006). *The Presidential Committee for analyzing the Communist dictatorship in Romania. Final report*. Retrieved from https://www.wilsoncenter.org/sites/default/files/media/documents/article/RAPORT%20FINAL_%20CADCR.pdf

Trading Economics (n.d.) *Romania labor force participation rate*. Retrieved from https://tradingeconomics.com/romania/labor-force-participation-rate

Varga, Á. (1999). *Hungarians in Transylvania between 1870 and 1995*. Budapest: Teleki László Foundation. Original published in *Magyar Kisebbség* 3–4, 1998 (IV), 331–407

World Bank (2011). *Cities in Europe and Central Asia: Romania*. Retrieved from https://documents1.worldbank.org/curated/en/840631511940024165/pdf/121730-BRI-P154478-PUBLIC-Romania-Snapshot-print.pdf

World Bank (2018). *Romania: Systematic country diagnostic*. Retrieved from https://www.worldbank.org/en/country/romania/publication/romania-systematic-country-diagnostic

World Bank (2021a). *Labor force participation rate, female (% of female population ages 15–64) (modeled ILO estimate)–Romania*. Retrieved from https://data.worldbank.org/indicator/SL.TLF.ACTI.FE.ZS?locations=RO

World Bank (2021b). *Labor force participation rate, male (% of male population ages 15–64) (modeled ILO estimate)–Romania*. Retrieved from
https://data.worldbank.org/indicator/SL.TLF.ACTI.MA.ZS?locations=RO

World Bank (2022). *Unemployment, total (% of total labor force) (modeled ILO estimate)–Romania*. Retrieved from
https://data.worldbank.org/indicator/SL.UEM.TOTL.ZS?locations=RO

World Economic Forum (2017). *The global competitiveness report 2017–2018*. Retrieved from
https://www.weforum.org/reports/the-global-competitiveness-report-2017-2018

World Economic Forum (2019). *The global competitiveness report 2019*. Retrieved from https://www3.weforum.org/docs/WEF_TheGlobalCompetitivenessReport 2019.pdf

Yavetz, Z. (1991). An eyewitness note: Reflections on the Romanian Iron Guard. *Journal of Contemporary History*, 26 (3/4), 597–610

De Rosa, D. and Kim, S.-Y. (2018). *Romania: Thriving cities, rural poverty and a trust deficit*. Retrieved from
https://www.brookings.edu/blog/future-development/2018/06/05/romania-thriving-cities-rural-poverty-and-a-trust-deficit/

GREECE:

Greece and the Eurozone crisis: what are the reasons behind Greece's downfall, and why is the economy only recovering slowly?

Abstract   Greece, a small country of just under 11 million people in southern Europe, made history not only for being the cradle of Western civilisation and the birthplace of democracy, but also for experiencing the highest decline in GDP of any modern country going through a financial crisis. As a result of the high government debt and the huge account deficit that became apparent in 2010, Greece had to borrow over €320 billion between 2010 and 2015 from European and international authorities and private creditors. This massive bailout of the Greek economy–the biggest financial rescue in history–helped the country get back on its feet and significantly contributed to the stabilisation of the euro, but also led to a huge drop in GDP (-26% between 2008 and 2014), dramatic levels of unemployment, widespread poverty and social exclusion, and the exodus of hundreds of thousands (often highly-skilled) Greeks.

What this chapter covers: Greece, Eurozone crisis, European sovereign debt crisis, Global Financial Crisis, Greece, Greek economy, unemployment in Greece, labour mobility

Introduction

Before 2010, Greece was, for many, a relatively unimportant EU member state at the south-eastern periphery of Europe. With a population of less than 11 million, a remote location several thousand kilometres away from the geographical centre of Europe, and comparatively low GDP, it has never been a major pillar of the EU economy. The importance of Greece in the EU changed abruptly in 2010, when many feared that it would withdraw from the Eurozone, which would significantly harm the monetary union or even put the common currency, the euro, at risk.

Why did 'Grexit', Greece's potential exit from the Eurozone, become a widely discussed option after 2012, and what were the reasons behind it? Why did Greece have to borrow over €320 billion– around €30,000 per person–just between 2010 and 2015 to save the country from complete bankruptcy? And what where the reasons behind Greece's years-long recession (2008–2016), which was worse than in any other European country?

This chapter provides answers to all these questions (and more) by looking at the Greek economy from the 1990s until today. We will analyse the reasons behind Greece's high government-to-debt ratio, revealing that deep-rooted structural problems such as a low employment rate, early retirement options and generous pensions, high labour costs and a growing trade deficit, a sizeable (but often inefficient) bureaucracy as well as rampant corruption and a large shadow economy played a considerable role in Greek's crisis and its long-lasting recession. We conclude that, while countries like Spain also suffered tremendously during the Eurozone crisis, the Greek economy has not bounced back as fast as in many other EU countries due to a multitude of persisting deep-rooted structural problems.

The Greek economy in the 1990s and the early 2000s, and Greece's accession to the Eurozone in 2001

When Greece became a democracy in 1974, different parties started to emerge, which competed for support and votes from the population over the following decades. In order to increase their popularity with the electorate, the two parties that were alternatingly in power, the *Panhellenic Socialist Movement* (PASOK), founded by Andreas Papandreou, and the *New Democracy Party* spent lavishly on all kinds of policies that benefitted a wide range of voters. As a result, the 1980s and 1990s were the cradle of numerous new welfare policies and rising government debt, as expenditure consistently surpassed revenues in every year since the 1970s.[1] In other words, for decades, Greece accumulated budget deficits, which increased its GDP-to-debt ratio year by year. A positive effect of the lavish spending by the public sector was the booming economy, especially in the early 21st century. Between the early 1990s and 2008, the Greek economy was growing faster, on average, than the rest of the EU; especially between 2001 and 2008, the economy boomed, with real GDP growth reaching 3.9% p.a. on average (World Bank, n.d.) The year before the 2004 Athens Olympics, which triggered massive investment in and around the capital, the Greek economy displayed the second highest GDP growth in the EU, at 5.8%, only behind Ireland. Since much of the massive spending to finance Greece's bloated welfare state and the Olympics was funded by money the government borrowed nationally and internationally, the country's sovereign debt accumulated and posed a permanent burden. By 2008, the year when, for the first time in 14 years, Greece's GDP did not grow, Greek government debt has risen to 99% of GDP–a level considerably higher than the EU average of 70% (Alogoskoufis, 2012). Although the mountain of debt that Greece accumulated over the past decades only became a major political and economic issue in 2008, it had caused friction before. Already years before Greece joined the Eurozone in 2001, its government debt surpassed the maximum level set in the EU's Stability and Growth Pact (SGP), which was, at least on paper, the criteria for becoming a Eurozone member. In 2000, for example, Greece's debt-to-GDP ratio broke the 100% mark (reaching nearly 105% of GDP) and was well above the 60% permitted by the EU. Similarly, also Greece's account deficit, at 3.7% of GDP, did not meet the GSP's limit of 3% that year. Yet, because several other members of the Eurozone, including Germany, were suffering from a recession and an irregularly high budget deficit, Greece was nevertheless allowed to join the Eurozone in 2001, two years after the other member states.

A result of Greece adopting the euro as single currency in 2001 was rapidly falling interest rates. For the first time in Greece's

---

[1] 2016 was the first year when the government did not run a budget deficit since the 1970s.

modern history, the government (as well as its citizens) could borrow at very reasonable interest rates. Before joining the Eurozone, investing in Greece (e.g. by purchasing government bonds) was perceived as relatively risky because inflation was high, exchange rate fluctuations persisted, and because the Greek economy and currency were not considered very stable and reliable. However, the country's Eurozone membership catapulted its economy and currency to a considerably higher trust level. Perceived credit risk for investing in Greece plummeted in 2001, because Greece now shared the same currency as 11 other EU members states, among them Germany, which made investors believe that the EU would discipline Greece to keep its finances (such as its debt, inflation, and account deficit) under control. Sharing the same currency also made investors assume that in case of problems or even default (in other words, if the Greek government could not repay its debt), EU institutions and the Eurozone member states would support the Mediterranean country. These perceived backups of the Greek economy, despite rising debt and continuous budget deficits, lowered the risk for investment in Greece, for which the yield spread between Greek and German 10-year government bonds plummeted from over 1,100 (!) basis points in early 1998 to approximately 50 in 2001 (and even less in the following years), converging with the bond yields of its strong EU neighbours (Gibson et al., 2011). In other words, due to Greece's Eurozone membership and the lower credit risk this posed, long-term interest rates declined from nearly 25% in 1995 to around 5% between 2000 and 2010. This made borrowing large sums of money easier, both for the government and private investors. Encouraged by never-seen low interest rates, the Greek government continued its spending spree after 2000, raising wages and the minimum wage, increasing pension payments, spending more on education and healthcare, and handing out generous social welfare payments. As a result, from 2000 onwards, Greece social welfare expenditure surpassed the OECD average, ending up nearly 7% above the rest of the OECD in 2013 (28% vs. 21% of GDP, respectively) (Canikalp/Unlukaplan, 2017). Rising expenditures on labour not only increased Greece's social welfare spending, but also made the country's products more uncompetitive internationally, which increased Greece's trade deficit. This, in return, put more pressure on the government to borrow more from international banks and other lenders. When the global recession, triggered by the financial crisis, started to hit Greece in 2008, things got markedly worse, as the state's tax revenues dwindled. This was because Greece's two main industries, tourism and shipping, suffered from the declining numbers of international travellers, as millions of people around the world were no longer able to spend money on lavish holidays. Also, the service sector (on which the Greek economy is highly dependent) started to stumble because many private consumers had to cut down spending on services that were not absolutely necessary. This decrease in business activities and thus tax revenues for the government, coupled with rising unemployment and related expenditure, meant that the Greek government was under considerable pressure by 2009.

When the Greek government borrowed money from foreign creditors to fund its budget deficit after 2001, it did so under the following two assumptions: first, that money would always be easily available, and second, that interest rates would remain low (due to the easy availability of cheap money in the global financial system). Yet, with the collapse of the Lehman Brothers Bank in September 2008 and the financial crisis that spread from the US to nearly all countries around the world, the international banking system was turned upside down. As it became apparent that many Americans who had taken out subprime mortgages–a loan usually given to borrowers with below-average credit scores who do not qualify for regular 'prime' loans–many mortgage-backed securities (MBS) collapsed in value and banks started to show liquidity problems. Alarmed investors, who lost confidence in the excessive risk-taking banks had engaged in the years before the crisis, started to withdraw their money, which meant that less credit was available. Lending money was considered much riskier once the financial crisis had laid open the problems subprime mortgages and the modern lending system posed, and the toxic assets and bad loans led to huge financial losses for most American and European banks. As a result, banks and private investors often stopped lending money to people or governments that seemed likely to default on their loans. Also in

Europe, when the Great Recession spread, banks in the European centre (such as German or French banks) became less and less eager to lend funds to countries whose finances seemed out of control. This particularly affected countries in the European periphery such as Portugal, Spain, Italy, and Greece. Things got worse when the new Greek government, under George Papandreou, corrected its annual deficit from 5.0% to 7.7% in 2009 (which was later revised to 9.4%), confessing that the previous government had whitewashed the actual state of the economy and the rising debt, which was corrected from 99.6% to 115.1% of GDP (with a following revision to 126.8%) (IMF, 2010). Similarly, the predictions on the annual budget deficit for 2009 were raised by nearly 10% points, from 3.7% to 12.5 %, and reached a staggering 15.4% in 2009, with government debt standing at 127% the same year. A result of Greece's deception of its actual fiscal situation and its yearlong fiscal mismanagement was that its credibility plummeted while long-term interest rates (bond yields)–and thus borrowing costs–increased sharply. This was for both existing and prospective loans, meaning that Greece had to pay much more than expected just to serve its existing obligations. The solvency problems of many banks and the unwillingness of many private investors to lend money to Greece meant that it would be unlikely to borrow more to finance its growing budget deficit and to serve its debt. The situation got considerably worse in 2010 when American credit rating agency Moody's massively downgraded the Greek debt by four notches in June, with even lower ratings following thereafter. This degradation of Greek government bonds close to 'junk' status made the yields for Greek ten-year bonds skyrocket, surpassing pre-euro levels, with the yield spread between Greek and German debt increasing by approximately 3,300 basis points in early 2012. As a result, in 2012, the annual average yield on long-term Greek government bonds (meaning the long-term interest rate) reached 22.5%, up by nearly 500% from 2008, when it stood at 4.8% (Statista, 2021).

Due to the high risk, few investors were interesting in lending money to the (nearly) bankrupt Greece, meaning the government was faced with a looming liquidity crisis, as there was not enough cash available to keep the country going. This forced dramatic measures among the government.

There were only two real ways out of Greece's situation: first, to greatly reduce expenditure and to increase revenues so it could quickly serve its creditors amidst the new high interest rates, or second, to ask international organisations such as the International Monetary Fund (IMF), the European Central Bank, the Commission as well as EU member states and their banks for large credits to avoid complete bankruptcy. A third option that had existed before 2001 was no longer possible: to depreciate the local currency in order to make exports more competitive, to encourage investment (with money losing its value, people would invest in real estate, the stock market or businesses to keep their savings), and to make the debt smaller in value. Printing more money would furthermore allow the government to repay its debt in the devalued currency. However, Greece's Eurozone membership made devaluation impossible, as only the European Central Bank (ECB) in Frankfurt could issue money or set interest rates. In other words, Greece (like all other Eurozone members) lost autonomy over its currency and monetary policies, which meant that the Greek government could not implement larger fiscal policies to improve the situation. Thus, the only real option for Greece was to request bailout funding from other Eurozone members, EU institutions, and the IMF. In order to avoid bankruptcy, the Greek government approached several public institutions for bailout credit in 2010, which was eventually granted because of the general fear that Greece could otherwise leave the Eurozone, thereby dragging more member states (or possibly even the whole Eurozone) into deep fiscal problems (Gourinchas et al., 2016). Had Greece abandoned the euro, the value of the single currency would most likely have plummeted due to a loss in credibility among investors from all over the world. Thus, in order to save the common currency, the European Commission, the ECB, and the IMF issued a €110 billion bailout loan for Greece in May 2010. Due to severe public pressure–millions of European citizens and several country heads were against providing money to Greece, whose people were often perceived as not very industrious–the loan was only granted under the condition that Greece would implement a massive government spending cut and start austerity measures. In other words, Greece was saved in 2010 but only under the condition that it would greatly reduce its budget deficit and restructure its country immediately. Part of these austerity measures included structural reforms such as raising the retirement age, lowering pensions, reducing the number of civil servants, privatising previously state-owned enterprises (to generate revenue) and raising taxes. Reducing the number of government workers and cutting funding for public institutions like museums, hospitals, schools and universities, the government could furthermore decrease expenditure. On the other hand, this severe cut in employment contributed to the official unemployment rate going through the roof, reaching 27.4% in 2013 and hovering around 25% for years (Statista, 2022). Reducing social benefits and pensions, in addition, contributed to much less aggregate demand, so the Greek economy started to contract, leading to economic stagnation, and putting hundreds of thousand people out of work. By mid-2012, nearly one third of businesses in Athens' busy commercial districts had closed down, as many people could no longer afford to go shopping, because tourist numbers dwindled, and because thousands of Athenians had moved to areas with lower rent (Reuters, 2021).

Unemployment became increasingly widespread, and people lining up for a meal at soup kitchens in Athens became a normality from 2010 onwards. Yet, despite the socio-economic hardship the Greek population had to endure, austerity measures reduced the pressure on the government only briefly, mainly when Greek public companies got privatised. This is because reduced government spending and a contracting economy also meant that government revenues (e.g. from income tax, corporate tax, and VAT) dried up as business activities declined.

In other words, the imposed austerity measures, more than helping the Greek economy get back on its feet, triggered a vicious cycle of recession and high unemployment. As a result, already by 2012, Greece had to ask for a second rescue package, which was, at €130 billion, even higher than the first in 2010. Indebted with well over €350 billion (€240 billion from the two bailouts and an additional €116 billion from the government debt they had accumulated before 2010), and with an unemployment rate of over 25% in August 2012, the economic situation in Greece was all but rosy. What is more, in addition to being in the middle of an unprecedented economic and fiscal crisis, Greece also had to stem a new humanitarian crisis: homelessness and the risk of poverty and social exclusion (especially among children) increased dramatically, and suicide figures skyrocketed, increasing by a whopping 300% between 2010 and 2014, especially among women (Macrotrends, n.d.) Hundreds of thousands of people, including those previously considered middle class, had to rely on food donations and soup kitchens. Relative health declined, both from a lack a balanced, nutritious diet, and from decreased public health spending (Vandoros et al., 2013).

A result of the dwindling economic activity in Greece was that the country's GDP contracted by over a quarter (26%) between 2008 and 2015. In 2011 and 2012 alone, GDP declined by 10.1% and 7.1%, respectively. While the government managed to reduce government expenditure due to severe spending cuts, the contracting economy meant that despite these austerity measures, Greece's debt-to-GDP ratio remained high and even increased between 2009 and 2017, from 127% to 179%. Despite a 50% debt 'haircut' on privately-owned debt (with private banks that held Greek bonds losing around €100 billion through the Greek debt restructuring) in 2011, Greece did not manage to pay some of its credit obligations in 2015 (specifically €1.6 billion to the IMF), making it the first country in history to default on an IMF loan. In fact, in 2015, Greece needed another bailout loan, this time for €86 billion. Despite the government having enacted 12 rounds of tax increases and implementing spending freezes and structural reforms between 2010 and 2016, Greece still suffers from high debt even today. As of 2021, it remains one of the top three most indebted countries globally, having served less than €50 billion of its debt obligations since 2010.

Several questions arise from the dire economic situation in Greece, which does not seem to be improving significantly: Why did the Greek economy contract so sharply? Why does unemployment remain high? What are the reasons that Greek governments have accumulated such high sovereign debt over the years? Was the euro a major factor contributing to the Greek crisis? We will argue that, while Eurozone membership certainly played a role because it removed the state's fiscal autonomy and possibility to implement independent fiscal policies (e.g. devaluating the currency by printing more money), it is far from being the main cause of the crisis. Eurozone membership allowed Greek governments to cover up its fiscal problems and to borrow at an unprecedented scale, but the major reasons for the country's economic downfall between 2008 and 2015 are long-lasting structural problems. While some improvements have been made, several of Greece's structural issues, such as a low (female) employment rate, early retirement age, low productivity and declining international competitiveness, rising trade deficits, generous pensions, a large civil sector, relatively low educational attainment, widespread nepotism and corruption, an inefficient bureaucracy, a large shadow economy and considerable welfare spending still persist.

In the following, we will analyse several structural problems Greece has faced for decades, assessing to what extent they have contributed to the fiscal disaster in 2010 and the following Great Recession, and investigating to what degree such problems have been overcome through Greece's austerity measures.

Why could Greece no longer borrow money easily after 2010? The step by many banks to not provide additional funding to countries like Greece was due to two main factors: first, compared to the pre-crisis years, money was no longer readily available, as banks around the world lost trillions of euros during the financial crisis, making them less solvent. Second, the risk of lending money to Greece, which was hit by a regression and rising unemployment, was perceived as comparatively high. As a result, Greece was not able to finance its debt–meaning to serve the monthly or annual payments to its creditors–by early 2010.

Abenomics vs. austerity: The Japanese approach to reviving the economy stands in sharp contrast to Greece's. Although Japan has high levels of sovereign debt (in fact, the Japanese government debt has surpassed Greece's for decades), the Japanese government under Prime Minister Shinzo Abe allocated massive funds for public works since

2013. The ideas behind this part of the Abenomics approach is that in times of recession, increased government spending could trigger economic growth, which in turn should make private people and corporations invest and spend more money. Abenomics follows an approach propagated by economist John Meynard Keynes, who advocated his idea of countercyclical fiscal policies (like higher government spending or lower taxes) during a recession to spur economic growth back in the 1930s.

Greece's structural problems

1) Thriving shadow economy & considerable tax evasion

The shadow economy (also referred to as the black market or the underground economy) exists in all countries, but among developed countries, it is especially notable in southern and south-eastern Europe (Medina/Schneider, 2018). Out of all 12 OECD countries assessed in 2017, Greece stands out for its thriving shadow economy, whose value was estimated at 21.5% of GDP (ILO, n.d.). Of course, as activities take place underground and therefore remain unreported, the actual scale is unclear. Yet, estimations are a good base to try to understand why some countries (such as Greece, but also other southern European countries like Italy and Spain) have a comparatively active parallel economy while countries like the US, Japan and Switzerland seem to suffer less from illegal business activities and tax evasion. Several factors, such as a country's history and culture, efficiency of and trust in government, deterrence and penalties, and the ease of complying with legal requirement for doing business (such as doing a correct tax declaration, for example) impact the scale of the shadow economy. According to research by the IMF, one of the biggest factors that positively correlates with the existence of large shadow economies and corruption is the weakness of civil administration in heavily regulated economies

(Medina/Schneider, 2018). In other words, countries that have complicated rules and regulation regarding business activities, but where the bureaucracy is not competent or efficient enough to enforce compliance with the regulations, are most prone to having a large shadow economy. This is the case in Greece, where the system of establishing a business or declaring taxes is relatively convoluted and time-intensive, but where government authorities do often not have the manpower, determination, and technical means to enforce stricter compliance with the law. In many cases, even if people are caught for their wrongdoings, corrupt members of the bureaucracy, judiciary, and police, who accept bribes to cover up the misconduct, has made the Greek government's efforts to curb illegal business activities largely ineffective.

While there is no clear definition of a shadow economy, it generally includes both illegal activities (such as trading stolen goods, drug dealing and drug manufacturing, prostitution and human trafficking, smuggling, gambling and fraud) and unreported income from exchanging goods and services. In other words, "the shadow economy comprises all economic activities that would generally be taxable were they reported to the tax authorities" (Schneider/Enste, 2002). Yet, the fact that millions of transactions remain unreported means governments around the world are losing trillions of dollars per year to the shadow economy.

> What is part of the shadow economy?
> Undeclared earnings from illegal activities, bribery money, undeclared labour and business transactions that do not follow legal procedures and are not taxed.

What exactly constitutes part of the shadow economy? Let us look at some examples of petty and more serious crimes that classify as part of the parallel economy. It could be letting a room on a vacation platform such as Airbnb and not paying taxes on the income, driving an unlicensed taxi after work without declaring the revenue, not providing customers in a bar with a receipt (and thus hiding the income from the tax man), repairing someone's car as barter, offering counsel and support (e.g. legal advice or tutoring) and getting paid in cash without reporting the fees as income, or selling drugs. Other activities may include asking for bribes (e.g. as a doctor in a hospital in exchange for better or faster treatment, or as a policeman when noticing irregular activities) that, due to their illegal nature, are also not reported to the tax authorities. As one can see, the nature of illegal business activities is very varied, and there are thousands of possibilities for how someone could evade paying taxes. Even simple acts such as paying someone to clean your home on a regular basis could potentially be part of the shadow economy.

Tax evasion (illegal non-payment or underpayment of taxes) poses the largest share of the Greek shadow economy. The most common types of tax evasion concern personal income tax, corporate tax, and VAT. One reason for the comparatively high share of tax evasion is Greece's widespread self-employment. For people running their own business, it is considerably less difficult to underreport income or to declare personal expenses as business expenses. Around one third (34%) of all workers in Greece were self-employed in 2017 (this ratio is among the highest in the world), meaning evasion of income taxes is considerably higher than in other EU member states. Also, corporate taxes paid by small businesses often remain underreported, as several small business owners (such as hairdressers, café and small shops owners or tutors) often refrain from providing receipts for cash payments (ILO, 2016). Several estimates put the figures of Greek businesses committing tax offenses as high as 50% in 2018, which reveals how rampant tax evasion is, and, while small businesses are more engaged in tax evasion, all kinds of Greeks businesses have been misreporting their taxes. So, it might be more difficult for regular company employees and pensioners to evade taxes, but small business owners and self-employed persons have real chances to underreport their income, and it takes considerable effort from the tax offices to reveal such wrongdoings.

How do we know that probably hundreds of thousands of self-employed Greeks evade taxes? Conducting interviews and asking Greeks whether they misreported their income would certainly not lead to the desired results. One way of assessing whether people correctly reported their income is to look at all declared revenues in Greece. Data from 2014 reveals that over five million Greeks–68.9% of all total taxpayers–reported an income range of €0-12,000 p.a. (Georgakopoulos, 2016). In fact, the mean income of the 64% of self-employed people who allegedly made below €12,000 was just €4,300 per year, or €358 per month. Another 29.5% declared their income to range between €12,000 and €42,000 per year. In other words, a whopping 98.4% of all Greek taxpayers were earning below €42,000 according to official data, with a mere 1.6% declaring an income over €42,000 (Georgakopoulos, 2016). While the economic situation of millions of Greeks did not look rosy in 2014, it is highly unlikely that over two thirds of the population made below €12,000 a year, which is not even enough for a one-person household to lead a comfortable life. It is also close to impossible that only 1.6% of all Greeks–a mere 120,000 people–earned over €42,000 (with just 200 people declaring an income of €500,000 and more), as Greece is home to many wealthy families, such as those in the shipbuilding and shipping business. Official reports put the number of millionaires in Greece at over 72,000 people (a figure about two thirds of the number of people with a declared income of over €42,000) (Credit Suisse Research Institute, 2021). While not all millionaires necessarily have a high income, it is very unlikely that with so many wealthy Greeks, the number of people with an income over €42,000 p.a. is just around 120,000.

A study by researchers from the University of Chicago (2012) took a different approach to revealing tax evasion, looking at the total declared revenue of several groups of self-employed professionals (such as lawyers, private tax accountants, financial advisors, doctors, and dentists), and checking the monthly mortgage obligations these groups had to serve (Artavanis et al., 2012). Their aim was to find out whether their income was in good relation to their monthly mortgage payments. Their analysis highlighted that if the reported income of self-employed lawyers, doctors, and accountants, among others, was true, most of them would spend more than 100% of their monthly salary to pay off their mortgage debt. Even considering that some of them probably have spouses who contribute to the mortgage obligations or the household budget, it is very unlikely that the monthly income was reported correctly (otherwise they would be left with very little money for other expenses such as food, travel, transportation, telecommunication, and hobbies, among others). Thus, the study impressively revealed that many self-employed high-income professionals tweaked the figures and considerably unreported their revenues. The cases analysed do not seem to be exceptions, as other studies show that even in later years, when tax evasion was more difficult, an average of seven out of ten self-employed people underreported their income (Christides, 2012). The study also highlighted that tax evasion is most rampant among doctors, who, on average, have an income 2.5 times higher than reported–while for all self-employed people, the average is 1.92 of the reported income.

The following figures reveals the extent of the problem of tax evasion among self-employed professionals: according to Artavanis et al. (2012), tax evasion by self-employed professionals alone amounted to €28 billion in 2009, equalling 10% of the Greek GDP that year (Inman, 2012). In other words, had only the self-employed Greeks paid the correct amount of taxes, the country's budget deficit would have been 31% lower in 2009. While people of all professions are engaged in tax evasion, with millions of Greeks underreporting their wealth, it has become apparent that misreporting of income substantially increases with wealth, according to the German magazine Der Spiegel (2010). While the exact size of the shadow economy and tax evasion remains unclear, several studies suggest that, between 2000 and 2020, it hovered between 8 and 11% of GDP (Athanasios, 2020). The largest shares are likely from personal income tax evasion (amounting to around 1.9–4.7% of annual GDP) and VAT evasion (equalling 3.5% of GDP) (Georgakopoulous, 2016). According to the European Commission's VAT GAP 2019 report, Greece has the second largest VAT gap in the EU, meaning it is the country with the second largest difference between potential VAT takings and the actual VAT payment receipts. Greece loses 25.8%– or close to €6 billion–of potential VAT to tax evasion (European Commission, Directorate-General for Taxation and Customs Union, 2021). Although the VAT gap in Greece is in decline, it is nearly twice as high as the EU average, and much higher than in countries like Croatia (1.0% VAT gap) and Sweden (1.4.%). Around half of the evaded VAT is due to a lack of receipts for transactions (such as for goods in small shops, restaurants, cafés and bars, or for different services), with the other half arising from customs fraud (e.g. importing goods from abroad with incorrect papers, claiming a lower value).

Why is tax evasion so common in Greece? The reasons behind this illegal but widely practiced custom are manifold and include people both willingly and unknowingly underreporting their income. In the following, we will look at the five main factors.

Greek politicians often describe tax evasion as a national sport. Indeed, there is even a short movie with the same title directed by Kelly Sarri, which highlights the enthusiasm, or even pride, some people develop for hiding income from the government. Greeks usually refer to tax evasion's long history, pointing out that it has always been a vital part of Greek culture. Thus, it can be argued that one reason for the underreporting of income is cultural, stemming back to the long-held tradition of hiding income from the taxman. Knowing that large numbers of Greeks underreport their income creates a free-rider effect. The rationale is that, although people might be willing to pay (the right amount of) taxes, knowing that others cheat makes them refrain from being honest, as they do not want to be the ones losing out while others take advantage. As it is generally well known among the Greeks that millions, especially the wealthy upper class, evade taxes, other people might feel discouraged to pay the correct amount of taxes because they do not understand why they should give up a large share of their income when others (such as well-known stars) largely keep their money. In other words, having others not comply with the tax law creates disincentives and unwillingness among the Greek population to let go of a considerable share of their income by paying the right amount of taxes.

Another reason for the vast spread of tax evasion is a general mistrust of the government and the tax authorities and an unwillingness to support these institutions, which are often considered inefficient and corrupt themselves. In other words, many

Greeks argue that they do not pay (the right amount of) taxes because they firstly do not trust the government and the bureaucracy, and secondly, because they do not see that the billions of euros in tax contributions are spent effectively. A third reason is that people find taxes too high, arguing that if they do not underreport their income they will not have enough to live on (comfortably), and pointing out that they do not think the government deserves such high tax contributions.

While tax rates are relatively high in Greece–VAT for example is a whopping 24%–they are part of the hen and egg dilemma: people not willing to pay the correct amount of taxes (which they consider 'too high') results in the government having to raise the tax rate even further to make up for the loss from tax evasion. In other words, as the pool of people paying taxes shrinks, those who comply with the law are faced with an even higher tax burden, despite receiving minimal social welfare benefits. Would all people pay the right amount of taxes, the Greek GDP would be up to 10% bigger every year, meaning that tax rates could be reduced rather than increased.

A fourth reason for widespread tax evasion is that getting caught is not shameful to many Greeks as tax evasion is, in general, not necessarily regarded as contemptible. Being caught does often not entail hefty fines, and in many cases, the tax offenders bribe the tax collectors or other officials so that they refrain from reporting them. In other words, because the penalties are neither shameful nor harsh, few people are disincentivised from paying taxes.

Lastly, it should not go unmentioned that some people unknowingly pay fewer taxes than required because of confusion regarding the (often very complicated and complex) Greek tax system and the lack of an easy electronic tool to calculate one's taxes. Some Greeks might be confused over what taxes to pay or get discouraged by the time-intensive system of filing one's taxes correctly. Mistakes potentially arise due to the complexity of the system, meaning that some people might unwillingly (and unknowingly) underreport their income and thus do not pay the correct amount of taxes. This share, however, is probably negligible.

2) Widespread nepotism & bribery

Another factor that has contributed to Greece's structural problems is widespread nepotism and bribery. Bribery not only limits the government's revenues, but also results in those who have the best connections or who bribe the most being often in charge of responsible work. While in Japan, for example, access to government-related jobs is highly restricted because applicants must pass centralised exams to become civil servants, personal connections often play a major role in Greece. This can be described as a form of nepotism, which describes favouritism granted to family and friends. Nepotism undermines the system of meritocracy, where the brightest and most talented become leaders in various fields and leads to positions often not being filled with the right people. The result is that productivity, efficiency, and innovation among companies or institutions might decline, potentially ending in apathy among workers. Having people in government and the bureaucracy who are neither educated nor motivated to do the job, but got the position due to nepotism, could also lead to decreased trust of and respect for state institutions. In fact, only 14% of all Greeks expressed trust in the parliament in 2020–a figure over three times lower than the OECD average. Also the Greek civil service (44%) and government (41%) receive below average ratings (OECD, 2021). It thus comes as no surprise that a commonly cited reason for the surge in highly skilled Greeks leaving the country after 2010 was widespread nepotism, which makes it difficult for well-qualified candidates to get a good job or to advance their career, as others with better connections might be promoted or hired instead. Some people even argue that nepotism makes "Greece intellectually and socially locked into its past" (Pine, 2019).

Bribery is another important factor for Greece's structural problems, as frequently occurring bribes have negative impacts on society and the economy. For one, it reduces trust in institutions, such as the bureaucracy, the healthcare system or tertiary education, if politicians, civil servants, doctors, and professors willingly accept bribes. This leads to distrust of the country's leading organisations or professions and can evoke a feeling of hopelessness regarding the future of one's country. Also, similar to nepotism, bribes could lead to people being in professions (e.g. chief medical staff) or with a license (e.g. driving license) for which they are not qualified, which could harm the health and safety of others. Bribing doctors to treat some patients sooner than others, e.g. for difficult surgery, could eventually even mean that those with the most urgent medical condition do not receive treatment first, which could end fatally for some. In addition, bribes could negatively impact the environment, e.g. if a company receives construction permission because of a bribe without closely checking the environmental impact. Bribing public officials to get around certain rules for businesses could lead to unfair competition, reducing business chances for others. Furthermore, bribery money, as it is off the radar, is also not taxed, reducing the government's revenue.

While Greek law forbids bribery, petty corruption remains a common phenomenon. In 2009, just before the crisis started to evolve in Greece, an estimated 13% of all households paid bribes in form of *fakelaki* (a small envelope with cash donations), amounting to €787 million in corruption payments executed only by private people that year (Der Spiegel, 2010). Bribes by businesses–mainly to government-related institutions or politicians to speed up processes or to get around bureaucratic rules or to receive favourable treatment–accounted for another €1 billion that year, according to the estimate by Transparency International (Der Spiegel, 2010). Petty corruption is especially common among the public sector, with hospitals, tax offices and construction-licensing bodies occupying the first three places in the corruption index. In 2017, Greek health minister Pavlos Polakis claimed that as many as 80% of doctors at public hospitals accepted bribery payments. He even proposed that "20% [of doctors] will not touch the patient if they will not get money" (Without Author, 2017). The impact on the Greek population is potentially enormous, as people might not have been able to provide such payments during the height of the Greek crisis, meaning that they might not have received the best treatment. While both the number of households paying bribes and the amount inside the *fakelaki* decreased during the recession and fell below the 500 million mark in 2012, the 2012 National Survey on Corruption revealed it is still a widespread problem in Greece that aggravates the country's structural problems (Transparency International, 2012). In 2020, Greece was ranked 59th in Transparency International's *Corruption Perception Index* (2020), perceived to be more corrupt than Malaysia and Namibia. This low rank reveals how severe and widespread tax evasion, bribery, and nepotism are perceived to be. All these illegal activities have not only greatly reduced the Greek government's annual revenue for decades, but also damaged trust in public institutions, encouraged emigration of highly-skilled people, and made government and the bureaucracy often sluggish and inefficient.

3) Greece's comparatively large public sector

Public sector employment has long been among the top jobs for many. Not only is employment as civil servant well paid, with generous pensions and long paid vacations, but jobs are generally for life. What is more, being a civil servant, for many, is seen as one of the least stressful professions, as the employment cannot be terminated easily from the employer's side. Before the Eurozone crisis, the Greek public sector grew steadily, both as a favour to voters and due to nepotism, meaning family members or close friends of influential people or members of the government got additional jobs in the civil sector. At the end of 2009, the number public servants reached nearly 693,000 (European Foundation for the Improvement of Living and Working Conditions, 2016). In addition to the comparatively large size of the public sector, civil servants were paid handsomely for their work: not only were both salaries and pensions high, but they automatically rose every year, and civil servants received a 13th and 14th salary (one month salary was added to their payment in December, for Christmas, with two 50% payments around Easter and the holiday period). In addition, several options for early retirement existed.

Greece's crisis and the long-term recession opened many people's eyes to the unsustainability of this level of generosity. Both due to internal and external pressure (from among the Greek private business community, but mainly from Greece's international creditors), the number of civil servants was reduced by 18%

between 2009 and 2015, from 693,000 to 567,000. While this posed a considerable effort to reduce fiscal expenditure, Greece's public sector still employed around 18% of the labour force in 2015, a figure considerably higher than that of Japan (5.9%), Germany (10.6%), Italy (13.6%) and the United States (15.3%) (OECD, 2021). Recent estimates by the International Labour Organization put the size of the civil sector even higher, showing that, despite the Greek government's spending cut, a considerable share of employees still work on the government's dime. Estimates by the Hellenic Federation of Enterprises (SEV) put the figure as high as 770,000 in 2016, leading them to argue that the public sector is "bloated" (European Foundation for the Improvement of Living and Working Conditions, 2016).

Due to these different estimates, there is no absolute certainty about how much of the GDP is spent on public sector employment. The most reliable source, the State General Accounting Office, suggests that the total overall government wage expenditure stood at €21,447 billion in 2015–a considerably lower figure than for 2009, where it was €31,013 billion. Yet, as GDP contracted, the share of public wages in relation to GDP remains considerable and still amounted to 12.2% of GDP in 2015. Due to the considerable reduction of the number of public servants (-18% between 2009 and 2015), pay freezes and lower salaries for new employees, net expenditure for public wages reached a level comparative to other EU countries, and was even 0.2 % below the EU average in 2015 (European Foundation for the Improvement of Living and Working Conditions, 2016).

It is fair to say that the large civil sector, with its generous remuneration, social benefits and high pensions contributed to the high budget deficit in the years before the crisis and so was an important factor in why Greece accumulated such high debt levels. While expenditure for public sector employment has been declining, a lack of finances still means that the relatively large Greek bureaucracy makes repaying the country's debt a challenge.

4) Generous state pensions & early retirement

Further structural problems that contribute to Greece's high annual budget deficits and government debt are its previously generous state pensions and early retirement policies. If, for example, a job is deemed arduous and unhealthy, Greek workers could retire at 50–at full pension. Professions considered arduous and unhealthy include hairdressers, trombone players, announcers and pastry chefs, which makes one wonder if this system is not antiquated and, in some respects, random. Even in other occupations, early retirement was often the norm; Greek male public servants can retire already at 58 if they have served for 35 years. A result from this past practice (as well as because of the generally low employment rates in Greece) was that just over 40% of Greeks aged 55 to 64 were employed in 2011. The figures during the Great Recession were even more worrisome, with a record low of 33.9% in 2015–well below the 52% EU average for that year (Eurostat, 2021). The generous Greek state-funded pension system has allowed hundreds of thousands of people to enjoy life in their fifties, often receiving substantial 'hardship allowances' in the past, which contributed to the rising expenses for national old-age pensions. For many years, public pensions in Greece were among the most generous in the EU, especially for its well-paid workers, placing a heavy burden on public finances (OECD, 2019). The share of pension expenditure in relation to GDP was higher than in other EU member states and even despite Greece's dramatic reduction of pension benefits as part of their international loan obligations after 2010, the share of expenditure on pensions remains the highest in the EU, surpassing 16% in 2018 (Eurostat, 2020). This figure was 4% points higher than the EU average, and around a third higher than pension spending in Sweden and Germany, standing at (11% and 12% of GDP, respectively).

Although state expenditure for pensions and early retirement is high, poverty and social exclusion during old age in Greece is relatively widespread. This is because pensions are distributed unequally, with those who had a well-paid job receiving considerably more than the rest. 69% of pensioners, for example, only receive 14% of average earnings, which increases the risk of poverty and social exclusion among the elderly (Ebbinghaus, 2021).

While the pension system in Greece was reformed in 2008 (with one result being that less than 10% of all Greek workers will be able to retire before they turn 65), expenditure for old-age pensions is still very high in Greece and has, for years, contributed to Greece's economic crisis.

5) Greece's low employment rate

For decades, or even centuries, Greece has been grappling with low employment figures. While the Greek employment rates were especially low during the recession, hitting rock bottom in late 2013 with less than half (48.5%) of all Greeks aged 15–64 in employment, low employment figures have been part of Greece's structural problems for a long time. Even during the economic boom years of 2001–2008, employment, which grew from 56% in 2001 to 61.5% in 2008, was well below many EU-15 countries (Federal Reserve Economic Data, 2021). In 2019, at a time when the Greek economy had already started to grow again, employment in Greece still stood at a lowly 61.2%–the lowest in the EU–, well behind not only countries like Sweden (82.1%), Germany (80.6%) and the Netherlands (80.1%), but also lagging behind historically more conservative countries with low employment rates for women like Portugal (76.1%) and Romania (70.9%) (Eurostat, 2020a). Even Italy, the other EU member state with an extremely low labour force participation rate among women and the youth, surpassed Greek levels, standing at 63.5%.

The main reason for the low employment rate is the below-average inclusion of women into the workplace. Although the female employment rate rose by about 10% between 1990 and 2020, currently not even half (49%) of all Greek women aged 20 to 64 work–a figure 18% lower than the EU average in 2018, and an astonishing 31% below Sweden (Eurostat, 2020c). Due to the female labour force participation rate, the Gender Equality Index 2021 ranked Greece a dismal second last in the EU in the work category (European Institute for Gender Equality, 2021).

Yet it is not only women that have a hard time getting a foot in the door when it comes to securing well-paid, regular employment in Greece. Labour force participation is also low among the youth. Even today (November 2021), nearly 15 years after the financial crisis started to hit Greece, the official youth unemployment rate is close to 40% (39.1.%)–10% above the country with the second largest youth unemployment, Spain (29.2%). Even before the crisis, in 2008, nearly three quarters (72%) of all Greeks aged 15 to 29 were economically inactive (Tubadji, 2012). While this lack of active involvement is not bad per se (good education can economically pay off for both the state and the people), the figure is telling for the low activity rate of people of all ages in Greece.

6) Low competitiveness & rising trade deficit

Countries are competitive if they produce goods others desire at a good price. For decades, Greece has suffered because the country neither had a strong production base nor was it able to export a substantial share of its goods and services. While Greek olives and olive oil are well known around the world, even in that area, trade volumes are minimal compared to olive oil from Italy and Spain. There are few Greek products apart from olives and oil that people in foreign countries use on a regular basis. This is not only because of Greece's dependence on the service sector (including tourism), which poses over 73% of employment, but also because most Greek products have not been very competitive on the world market (Statista, 2021). One reason are the high labour costs, which have risen substantially since the 1990s, making Greek products relatively expensive. If we compare the rise in labour costs for German employers and their Greek counterparts over the past decades, we can see that while in politicians in Germany tried to keep labour costs at a rather constant level in the 1990s and early 2000s by restricting pay increases for several years, labour costs in Greece rose considerably between 1990 and 2008 (Joebges et al., 2021). By 2010, Greece had the second highest nominal unit labour costs based on hours worked in the EU (Eurostat, 2022b). The main reasons behind the rising wages were not only Greece's relatively high inflation, but also pressure from labour unions and workers demanding higher salaries. In order to please working-class voters, politicians gave in to their demands. Yet, while this move raised the living standards in Greece, higher labour costs resulted in more expensive, less competitive Greek products on the world market. Before the introduction of the single currency, Greece could (and often did) devalue the Greek drachma to raise the competitiveness of its goods, but such measures were not possible once they joined the Eurozone in 2001. This means that in the 21st century, Greek products lost their competitive edge, increasing the country's trade deficit. In 2008, for example, the trade balance of goods was hugely negative, at around $44 billion–or 12.6% of GDP (Macrotrends, n.d.) In fact, since the 1960s (or even further back), Greece has imported more than it exported, which highlights the long-term nature of this structural problem.

While a negative trade balance is not necessarily bad, the low productivity and comparatively high wages in Greece have lowered the chances of Greek products being sold abroad. By investigating the labour productivity per employed person in different EU countries, it is obvious that Greece has not yet managed to improve its workers' productivity. In 2020, productivity per employed person an hour stood at 66.5 (with 100 being the EU average in 2020) (Eurostat, 2022b). This was not only well below Greece's result from 2013, when it was over 80, but also nearly four times lower than that of Sweden, for example. Even compared to the average EU rating of 100 in 2020, Greece's productivity is dismal.

7) Emigration & brain drain

High youth unemployment, widespread nepotism (implying fewer chances for talented, but less well-connected people to land a good job), low wages and rampant poverty are only some factors that contributed to the fact that millions of Greeks live outside the country. Aggravated by the economic crisis and the country's long-term recession, between 2008 and 2015 alone, 427,000 predominantly young and often well educated citizens left the country according to estimates by the Greek Central Bank (Deutsche Welle, 2016). During the height of the crisis, in 2013 and 2014, the number of young professionals or recent graduates migrating to foreign shores (especially Germany, the UK and the UAE) even surpassed 100,000 per annum. The recent waves of labour migration have made Greece rank second after Spain in regard to the proportion of young people emigrating.

Emigration dates back centuries and there are around five million Greeks (equalling about half of the population inside the country) scattered around the world. A lack of economic opportunities has been the main driving force behind all waves of emigration, revealing Greece's deeply entrenched structural problems. The recent emigration wave during the Greek recession is probably the most worrisome, as the share of skilled and highly-skilled emigrants was considerably higher than during previous waves. Scholars even refer to the large labour mobility of young Greeks after 2008 as a 'brain drain', suggesting that Greece is harmed by the departure of hundreds of thousands of young, educated, and well-trained citizens.

One reason behind the fast rise of labour mobility from Greece to other EU countries is high youth unemployment, which spiralled from 2009 onwards. Already in 2009, the year the Greek crisis started to pick up speed, 13% of all Greeks aged 25–29 with a university degree and not currently in education were unemployed (OECD, 2011). In 2014, the figure was beyond 20%, and even in late 2020, 12.2% of all young Greeks with a degree were jobless, making their situation the worst in the whole EU (OECD, 2021). Their share is over twelve times higher than in Germany, which has contributed to many young Greeks' decision to move to this European economic powerhouse. However, it is not only unemployed Greeks that have looked for jobs in Germany or the UK. In fact, over half (52%) of recent mobile labourers leaving Greece were gainfully employed before their departure (Alcidi/Gros, 2019). Yet, many of them were underemployed (working fewer hours than wanted or in lower positions than their education would justify), on temporary contracts, or working for a low salary. Many others were unhappy with the lack of chances to get promoted to a position with higher responsibilities. Thus, since 2010, nearly half a million Greeks have looked for more opportunities in other countries, such as Germany and the UK, where salaries are considerably higher and where ample opportunities for professionals such as engineers, IT specialists and medical doctors (among many others) exist.

Why are the conditions so bad in Greece? Why do young Greeks find it hard to find good jobs? One reason for the high youth unemployment is that the transition from education to the labour market is difficult for many graduates, as companies look for people with training and experience, while Greek university education often remains predominantly theoretical. In other words, young graduates lack the practical knowledge and experience to compete with older workers. According to a McKinsey study (2014), the most common skills young graduates lack are hard skills such as English language proficiency and hands-on experience, usually gained through internships and training, but also soft skills like problem-solving skills, analytical skills, or even a proper work ethic (Mourshed et al., 2014).

The competition for jobs increased substantially during the height of the crisis as the Greek government had to reduce the number of civil servants, putting a hiring freeze in place for years. Private enterprises also had to reduce their headcount due to their often dismal economic performances during the long recession, where demand for goods and services plummeted. For companies, it was the most cost-efficient option to make young workers redundant because the sunken costs were lowest for them–meaning that the companies had invested the least in younger workers for their training. As a result, the youth unemployment rate rose at a higher rate than general unemployment during the crisis.

However, not only the poorly functioning labour market in Greece is to blame for low youth employment. Another dominant reason is the skill mismatch, with Greek universities producing too many graduates in humanities and social sciences and too few people in STEM subjects. As a result, the joblessness rate among highly-skilled youngsters is nearly as high as for low-skilled young Greeks–a real rarity in Europe. The problem does not only lie at the supply side, though. As Greece has a relatively low share of large international businesses (such as in manufacturing or technology), Greek talents often do not find the jobs they want. As previously discussed, Greece has the highest rate of self-employed people. In addition, micro firms with fewer than ten employees are widespread, accounting for as much as 97% of all firms in the country (European Commission, 2018). With over half (57.1%) of all jobs in Greece being generated in these micro firms in 2018, it is difficult for highly specialised workers (e.g. graduates with a PhD in physics, chemistry, engineering or neuroscience, for example) to find suitable work inside the country. All these factors have contributed to the large share of young, educated Greeks leaving their home country in the 2010s.

By analysing the background and educational attainments of these new mobile citizens, one can easily spot that the vast majority of recent emigrants from Greece have been highly educated. Among those with tertiary education, nearly 12% had a PhD and 50% a Master's degree (Alcidi/Gros, 2019). In addition, over half (52%) of all emigrants were employed during the six months before their departure, revealing that unemployment was not always the driver for emigration. When asked for their motivation, the most-cited reasons for their move abroad were corruption, the lack of a meritocracy, high levels of nepotism, a lack of opportunities for young workers, low salaries and limited chances for career development.

The high emigration rate of young, skilled professionals poses a serious danger to the country, as it loses a considerable share of talented people. A recent Greek migrant to Germany, Christos Christoglou, points out that it is "[u]sually the brightest, who can get a good job elsewhere, or the ones who could really offer something to the country [...] [that] leave the country" (Deutsche Welle, 2011). He concludes that this is a "huge disaster" because it means that mainly people with mediocre grades or degrees stay, probably impacting the country and its institutions in the future as the brightest have turned their back on Greece. if recent mobile citizens do not return, the chances that Greece will suffer from long-term brain drain (rather than benefitting from the brain circulation) are high. This could potentially have severe socio-economic repercussions, such as a fast-advancing ageing society and an even tighter budget for state pensions due to fewer workers paying into the social security system. In addition, a brain drain reduces the labour force and productivity and could decrease innovation and competitiveness of Greek companies. As previously stated, missing some of the most well-educated people could mean potential labour shortages in some professions (as is the case in the medical professions, where around 18,000 young doctors left Greece between 2010 and 2018), less revenue for the government, and fewer talents to lead the country.

While the number of mobile Greeks has declined in recent years, return mobility remains relatively low. Thus, there is a real chance that the hundreds of thousands of well-educated, open-minded Greeks that left during the great recession could remain in the diaspora long-term contributing to brain drain and the problems associated with it.

Conclusion

Greece's sovereign debt crisis and the following long-term recession changed the Greek peninsula and its people in many respects. Unemployment skyrocketed, leaving around half of the youth unemployed, and resulted in an employment rate of under 50%; in addition, poverty and homelessness reached previously unknown levels for an EU-15 country, and the Greek economy shrank by over a quarter. Many have pointed at the global banking system, the euro, and the harsh conditions imposed by the creditors (e.g. Germany and France) as the main culprits for Greece's tragedy. While these three factors certainly impacted the socio-economic development of Greece after 2008, this chapter has shown that the country's structural problems pose the main reason for Greece's massive economic decline.

This chapter analysed how structural problems impacted the country's financial and economic situation after 2008. The following three points seem to have had a considerable negative impact on Greece's dire performance after 2008: 1) Labour problems: e.g. a low employment rate, previously generous early retirement options, a bloated, inefficient bureaucracy with high compensation, and increasing brain drain; 2) Social issues: e.g. widespread tax evasion, nepotism, and bribes; 3) Trade & budget issues: e.g. Greece's low competitiveness and the resulting trade deficit that led to rising annual budget deficits and a fast growing debt mountain. It can be argued that, had Greece performed better in some of these categories, the recession would have been less severe and more short-lived. This is particularly true for the widespread tax evasion and bribery that have been rampant in Greece for decades or even centuries, as they have contributed significantly to the rising Greek budget deficit and had a severe impact on the collapse of the Greek economy.

External (and, to some extent, also internal) pressure, such as from the international creditors, has triggered change in Greece. Pensions were cut, the most generous early retirement policies scrapped, the public sector experienced a year-long hiring freeze, and stricter penalties and more serious efforts to curb tax evasion and bribery were enforced. In addition, labour market reforms were introduced, many state enterprises privatised, expenditure on public institutions such as schools, universities, hospitals, and museums severely cut, and the competitiveness of some industries increased. These efforts had tangible results: the annual budget went from a massive deficit of 15.1% in 2010 to a surplus of 1.1% in 2019, with the Greek economy growing in the years straight before the Covid-19 pandemic (Country Economy, 2021). Yet, many scholars and politicians argue that the reforms have not been fundamental or far-reaching enough to get Greece back on its feet and to support sustainable growth in the future. Due to the massive decline in GDP between 2010 and 2015, Greek debt levels have remained high. In fact, the Covid-19 pandemic and the resulting problems on the labour market (Greece highly depends on tourism, which collapsed during the pandemic) have propelled Greek's debt ratio to new heights, surpassing the 200% of GDP mark in 2020 and accounting to nearly $400 billion (Statista, 2021). As Greece suffers from paying billions in interest rates on their loans, returning their credits in due time is a real struggle. It will take Greece decades, if not centuries. In order to repay its debts, Greece needs to stem the remaining structural issues, above all increasing the employment rate es among women and the elderly. What is also important for the future of the country is to encourage highly skilled emigrants to return home so they can use their increased financial assets, their new skills and knowledge, and their international connections for their home country. If Greece does not succeed in keeping its brightest people in the country or in enticing the elite diaspora return, and if it fails to provide suitable employment for its well-trained university graduates and other skilled labourers, the future for Greece will be much less rosy than it could be. Yet, there is hope that the end of the Covid-19 pandemic could spur massive growth in the Greek tourist sector and support the overall well-being of the Greek economy.

References

Alcidi, C. and Gros, D. (2019). *EU mobile workers: a challenge to public finances?* Contribution for informal ECOFIN, Bucharest, 5–6 April 2019. Retrieved from https://www.ceps.eu/wp-content/uploads/2019/04/EU%20Mobile%20 Workers.pdf

Alogoskoufis, G. (2012). Greece's sovereign debt crisis: retrospect and prospect. *Hellenic Observatory Papers on Greece and Southeast Europe 54*, 1–51. Retrieved from http://eprints.lse.ac.uk/42848/1/GreeSE%20No54.pdf

Artavanis, N., Adair Morse, T. & Tsoutsoura, M. (2012). Tax Evasion Across Industries: Soft Credit Evidence from Greece. *Chicago Booth Paper, 12* (25), 1–53

Athanasios, A., Kalamara, E. and Charalampos, K. (2020). Estimation of the size of tax evasion in Greece. *Bulletin of Applied Economics, Risk Market Journals, 7* (2), 97–107

Canikalp, E. and Unlukaplan, I. (2017). Political determinants of social expenditures in Greece: an empirical analysis. *Public Sector Economics, 41* (3), 359–377 Retrieved from
http://www.pse-journal.hr/upload/files/pse/2017/3/canikalp_unlukaplan. pdf#:~:text=The%20share%20of%20social%20expenditures,%E2% 80%9Cpay%20as%20you%20go%E2%80%9D

Christides, G. (2012). Wealthy Greeks still don't pay taxes. *Spiegel International*, 1 November 2012. Retrieved from
https://www.spiegel.de/international/europe/wealthy-greeks-still-dodging-taxes-despite-crisis-a-864703.html

Country Economy (2021). *Greece government budget deficit 2021*. Retrieved from https://countryeconomy.com/deficit/greece

Credit Suisse Research Institute (2021). *Global wealth databook 2021*. Retrieved from https://www.credit-suisse.com/media/assets/corporate/docs/about-us/ research/publications/global-wealth-databook-2021.pdf

Der Spiegel (2010). Greek corruption booming, says Transparency International. *Der Spiegel*, 2 March 2010. Retrieved from
https://www.spiegel.de/international/europe/european-debt-crisis-greek-corruption-booming-says-transparency-international-a-681184.html

Deutsche Welle (2011). Greece loses skilled graduates to countries that are still hiring. *Deutsche Welle*, 9 August 2011. Retrieved from
https://www.dw.com/en/greece-loses-skilled-graduates-to-countries-that-are-still-hiring/a-15291125

Deutsche Welle (2016). Greece Central Bank reports 'brain drain' of 427,000 young, educated Greeks since 2008. *Deutsche Welle*, July 2, 2016. Retrieved from
https://www.dw.com/en/greece-central-bank-reports-brain-drain-of-427000-young-educated-greeks-since-2008/a-19373527

Ebbinghaus, B. (2021). Inequalities and poverty risks in old age across Europe: The double-edged income effect of pension systems. *Social Policy & Administration, 55* (7), 440–455

European Commission (2018). *2018 SBA fact sheet Greece*. Retrieved from https://ec.europa.eu/docsroom/documents/32581/attachments/13/ translations/en/renditions/native

European Commission, Directorate-General for Taxation and Customs Union (2021). *VAT gap in the EU: report 2021*. Brussels: Publications Office

European Foundation for the Improvement of Living and Working Conditions (2016). *Greece: reducing the number of public servants–latest developments*. Retrieved from
https://www.eurofound.europa.eu/publications/article/2016/greece-reducing-the-number-of-public-servants-latest-developments

European Institute for Gender Equality (2021). *Gender Equality Index: Greece*. Retrieved from
https://eige.europa.eu/gender-equality-index/2021/country/EL

Eurostat (2020a). *Europe 2020 employment indicators: Employment rate of people aged 20 to 64 in the EU reached a peak at 73.1% in 2019*. Retrieved from
https://ec.europa.eu/eurostat/documents/2995521/10735440/3-21042020-AP-EN.pdf/fc7e4ab2-85ef-c48a-ee8d-ef334d5c2b8

Eurostat (2020b). *Social protection statistics–pension expenditure and pension beneficiaries*. Retrieved from
https://ec.europa.eu/eurostat/statistics-explained/index.php?title=Social_protection_statistics_-_pension_expenditure_and_pension_beneficiaries#:~:text=The%20relative%20importance%20of%20expenditure,expenditure%20was%2015.8%20%25%20of%20GDP

Eurostat (2020c). *Women's employment in the EU*. Retrieved from
https://ec.europa.eu/eurostat/de/web/products-eurostat-news/-/EDN-20200306-1

Eurostat (2021). *Evolution of employment rate, 55 to 64 years, EU 2002-2020*. Retrieved from
https://ec.europa.eu/eurostat/statistics-explained/index.php?title=File:Evolution_of_employment_rate,_55_to_64_years,_EU,_2002-2020_(%25).png

Eurostat (2022a). *Labour productivity and unit labour costs*. Retrieved from
https://appsso.eurostat.ec.europa.eu/nui/show.do?dataset=nama_10_lp_ulc&lang=en

Eurostat (2022b). *Labour productivity per person employed and hour worked (EU27_2020=100)*. Retrieved from
https://ec.europa.eu/eurostat/databrowser/view/tesem160/default/table?lang=en

Federal Reserve Economic Data (2021). *Employment rate aged 15-64: all persons for Greece*. Retrieved from
https://fred.stlouisfed.org/series/LREM64TTGRQ156S

Georgakopoulos, T, (2016). *Tax evasion in Greece–a study*. Retrieved from
https://www.dianeosis.org/en/2016/06/tax-evasion-in-greece/

Gibson, H., Hall, S. and Tavlas, G. (2011). The Greek financial crisis: growing imbalances and sovereign spreads. *Bank of Greece Working Paper 124*, 1–42; Retrieved from
https://www.bankofgreece.gr/Publications/Paper2011124.pdf

Gourinchas, P.-O., Philippon, T. and Vayanos, D. (2016). The analytics of the Greek crisis. *NBER Macroeconomics Annual*, 31, 1–81

ILO (n.d.). *Diagnostic report on bogus self-employment in Greece and recommendations for reforms*. Retrieved from
https://www.ilo.org/wcmsp5/groups/public/---ed_emp/documents/projectdocumentation/wcms_531548.pdf

ILO (2016). *Diagnostic report on undeclared work in Greece*. Geneva: ILO

Inman, P. (2012). Primary Greek tax evaders are the professional classes. *The Guardian*, September 9, 2012. Retrieved from https://www.theguardian.com/world/2012/sep/09/greece-tax-evasion-professional-classes?CMP=twt_gu

International Monetary Fund (2010). Greece: Staff report on request for stand-by arrangement. *IMF Country Report, 10* (110), 1–144. Retrieved from https://www.imf.org/external/pubs/ft/scr/2010/cr10110.pdf

Joebges, H., Zwiener. R. and Albu, N. (2021). *Germany's struggle for price competitiveness Macroeconomic effects of wage and unit labour costs developments in Germany.* Retrieved from https://www.boeckler.de/pdf/v_2021_10_30_joebges.pdf

Macrotrends (n.d.). *Greece trade balance 1960-2022*. Retrieved from https://www.macrotrends.net/countries/GRC/greece/trade-balance-deficit

Macrotrends (n.d.). *Greek suicide rates 2000–2022*. Retrieved from https://www.macrotrends.net/countries/GRC/greece/suicide-rate#:~:text=Greece%20suicide%20rate%20for%202019,a%206%25%20decline%20from%202015

Medina, L. and Schneider, F. (2018). Shadow economies around the world: What did we learn over the last 20 years? *IMF Working Papers, 18* (17), 1–76

Mourshed, M., Patel, J. and Suder, K. (2014). *Education to employment: getting Europe's youth into work*. McKinsey Center for Government. Retrieved from https://www.mckinsey.com/~/media/mckinsey/industries/public%20and%20social%20sector/our%20insights/converting%20education%20to%20employment%20in%20europe/education%20to%20employment%20getting%20europes%20youth%20into%20work%20full%20report.pdf

OECD (2011). *Education at a glance 2011. OECD indicators*. Paris: OECD Publishing. Retrieved from https://www.oecd.org/education/skills-beyond-school/48631089.pdf

OECD (2019). *Pensions at a glance. OECD and G20 indicators*. Retrieved from https://www.oecd.org/els/public-pensions/PAG2019-country-profile-Greece.pdf

OECD (2021). *Education at a glance 2021. OECD indicators*. Paris: OECD Publishing.

OECD (2021). *Government at a glance 2021. Country fact sheet*. Retrieved from https://www.oecd.org/gov/gov-at-a-glance-2021-greece.pdf

OECD (2021). *Government at a glance 2021*. OECD Publishing: Paris

Pine, R. (2019). Nepotism, graft and apathy holding Greece back. *The Irish Times*, 23 April 2019. Retrieved from https://www.irishtimes.com/news/world/europe/nepotism-graft-and-apathy-holding-greece-back-1.3868503

Price Waterhouse Cooper (2016) *World tax summaries: Taxation in Greece. Corporate and individual taxes in Greece*. Retrieved from https://www.pwc.com/gr/en/publications/greek-thought-leadership/world-tax-summaries.html

Radoslaw A. and Zaidi, A. (2016). Risk of Poverty among older People in EU countries. *CESifo DICE Report, 14* (1), 37–46. Retrieved from https://www.ifo.de/DocDL/dice-report-2016-1-zaidi-antczak-march.pdf

Reuters (2012). Crisis shuts a third of shops in Athens city centre. *Reuters*, 25

September 2012. Retrieved from
https://www.reuters.com/article/us-greece-business/crisis-shuts-a-third-of-shops-in-athens-city-centre-idUSBRE88N0NW20120924?edition-redirect=ca

Schneider, F. and Enste, D. (2002). *Hiding in the shadows: the growth of the underground economy*. Washington: IMF

Statista (2017). *Where shadow economies are well established*. Retrieved from https://www.statista.com/chart/8015/where-shadow-economies-are-well-established/#:~:text=According%20to%20the%20IMF%2C%20heavily,regulated%20and%20efficient%20government%20institutions

Statista (2021). *Annual average yields on long-term government bonds in Greece from 2000 to 2020*. Retrieved from statista.com/statistics/576257/capital-market-interest-rate-greece-europe/

Statista (2021). *Greece: Distribution of the workforce across economic sectors from 2009 to 2019*. Retrieved from https://www.statista.com/statistics/276400/distribution-of-the-workforce-across-economic-sectors-in-greece/

Statista (2021). *Greece: National debt from 2016 to 2026*. Retrieved from https://www.statista.com/statistics/270409/national-debt-of-greece/#:~:text=In%202020%2C%20the%20national%20debt,Greece%20is%20currently%20ranked%20second

Statista (2022). *Greece: Unemployment rate from 1999 to 2020*. Retrieved from https://www.statista.com/statistics/263698/unemployment-rate-in-greece/

Transparency International (2012). *National Survey on Corruption in Greece*. Athens: Transparency International

Transparency International (2020). *2020 corruption perceptions index 2020*. Retrieved from https://www.transparency.org/en/cpi/2020

Tubadji, A. (2012). *Youth unemployment in Greece: Economic and political perspectives*. Berlin: Friedrich Ebert Foundation. Retrieved from https://library.fes.de/pdf-files/id/09475.pdf

Vandoros, S., Hessel, P., Leone, T. and Avendano, M. (2013). Have health trends worsened in Greece as a result of the financial crisis? A quasi-experimental approach. *European Journal of Public Health*, *23* (5), 727–731

Wichman, A. (2021). The Greek Diaspora Around the World. *Greek Reporter*, 6 March 2021. Retrieved from https://greekreporter.com/2021/03/06/greek-diaspora-around-the-world/

Without Author (2017). Health Minister claims 80% of doctors receive money under the hand. *Keep Talking Greece*, 6 November 2017. Retrieved from https://www.keeptalkinggreece.com/2017/11/06/greece-fakelaki-doctors/

World Bank (n.d.). *GDP growth (annual %)–Greece*. Retrieved from https://data.worldbank.org/indicator/NY.GDP.MKTP.KD.ZG?locations=GR

ITALY:

VI

The rise of the Mummy's Boys (*mammoni*): why do so many Italian live with their parents?

Abstract   In 2019, nearly three quarters of Italian males aged 18 to 34 lived with their parent(s), and the average age of young Italians moving out of the parental home has surpassed 30. While for a long time, the high youth unemployment rate was regarded as the main reason for Italians not leaving home sooner, recent data suggests that, in addition to economic factors and a saturated housing market, cultural norms and traditions play a major role, with many Italian mothers enjoying the company of their adult children. Rising wealth among middle-class families, where mothers have often been out of the labour market for decades, has led to many Italian mothers finding their calling in caring for their children well into adulthood, and has often made their sons dependent on their financial, emotional, and practical support. Yet, delayed departure from the family home can interfere with romantic relationships, delay marriage, lower fertility rates, and lead to a decline in the labour force participation of young Italians.

What this chapter covers   Italy, youth unemployment, precarious work conditions, mother-son-relationship in Italy, housing market, cohabitation between parents and child, Italy's mummy's boys, NEET in Italy

Introduction

Moving out of the parental home is considered a milestone or turning point for young adults, as it generally marks the transition to an independent life and is a sign of social and psychological maturity. In the EU, the age when children reach residential autonomy varies starkly, with Swedes leaving the parental home on average nearly 12 years earlier than Italian youngsters. The majority of Swedes move out after secondary school, aged 18.5, whereas the average Italian remains in the parental home until their 30th birthday (30.1 years) (Eurostat, 2019). This is not only because Italians tend to study in the town they are from and often commute to university from home but also because Italians often prefer to stay at 'Hotel Mamma' even after graduation. Looking at the share of young adults between 25 and 34 who still live with their parents, Italy, again, is among the top. Around 50% of Italians aged 25–34 live with their parents a figure 20% above the EU average, and 12 times higher than the figure for Denmark (Eurostat, 2020a).

The phenomenon of young adults staying with their parents has become so prevalent that several new terms have been coined. One is 'accordion family', which describes a multigenerational household–comprising of parents and their adult children–sharing the same roof. A more widespread terms specifically for sons staying in the parental home is '*mammoni*': mummy's boys. Just like the '*bamboccioni*' (big babies)–a pejorative word for Italian adult men cohabitating with their parents–, *mammoni* are heatedly discussed by politicians and in the news, with many people opposing delayed departure from the parental home, as it affects cohabitation with a romantic partner, marriage, and childbirth, and could negatively impact the labour force participation of young Italians.

The reasons for Italians leaving the nest considerably later than youngsters in most other European countries are manifold and can be traced back to economic, financial, social, and cultural factors. The lack of economic independence among many young Italians, who tend to graduate from university much later than their peers in other EU countries and who often neither have their own income during their studies nor receive financial support from the government, makes it hard for many university students to gain residential autonomy. In addition, the high youth unemployment and the prevalence of precarious work conditions among many young employees, whose salary is often not enough to be able to afford their own rental apartment, also contribute to the spread of accordion families. Other factors for low residential independence are high rents and a saturated housing market in most Italian cities, which have made it impossible for a large number of people in their 20s to rent a place on their own.

Financial reasons are central to explaining the rise of *mammoni*, but cultural reasons and social norms have equally strong explanatory powers for why many young Italians seem uninterested in leaving Hotel Mamma, where they not only live rent-free but also get cared for by their altruistic mothers, Yet, it often is not only the adult children, but also the mothers themselves who prefer this situation. In contrast to parents in most other European countries, the majority of Italian mothers express satisfaction with their situation and reveal that cohabitating with their grown-up children leaves them fulfilled. Manacorda/Moretti (2006) proposed that some parents even 'bribed' their children into prolonged cohabitation, incentivising their adult children to stay at home by transferring money to them and providing all the comforts of a hotel (e.g. meals, laundry service, room service), in addition to emotional support.

In this chapter, we will assess the main reasons for many young Italians' preference for cohabitation with their parents, showing that financial dependence, good parent-child relationships, and a certain degree of laziness among many adult sons are the main reasons for the late transition from the parental home to residential independence.

Economic reasons: delayed financial independence

Financial independence (or at least financial stability) is a prerequisite for people to become renters. In Italy, most youngsters achieve financial stability well after their peers in other EU member states. The four main reasons for this are: 1) structural, long-term high youth unemployment due to skill mismatches and a labour market favouring older people; 2) a tendency for precarious work conditions and low wages among young workers; 3) a high percentage of youngsters not in education, employment, or training (NEET); 4) general late entry into the labour market due to long periods at university and a bumpy transition between study and employment.

Over the past 20 years, the unemployment rate among Italians aged 15 to 24 has never been below 20%. Between 2013 and 2015, when Italy suffered the most from the impact of the global recession and the Eurozone crisis, youth unemployment even surpassed the 40% mark. As Liotti (2020) points out, the impact of the financial crisis was three to four times more severe for Italy's young adults than for more senior generations, mainly due to the lack of job security among many new employees. While the labour market has recovered gradually since then, youth unemployment in 2021 was still around 30%–about twice as high as the EU average (Destatis, n.d.) Even in recent years, in some of Italy's southern regions such as Sicily, Calabria and Campania, nearly half of the young population is officially looking for work but unable to find a job (Statista, 2021i). One reason can be found in the educational system, which is often described as antiquated and which has even received criticism from the OECD for not supporting students in getting practical skills. According to the 2015 PISA test, which measures 15-year-olds' performance in core competences like science, mathematics and reading, Italy ranked below the OECD average in two of the three categories (science and reading) and fared only average in mathematics (OECD, 2018b). Reasons for the weak performance of Italian students could be a chronic underfunding of the Italian education system, especially in the south, and a heavy focus on theory rather than practice in most schools. Due to a lack of attention to practical skills, including independent thinking, decision-making, self-determination, and PC literacy, transition from school to work is often slow in Italy, and those leaving high school without a degree have considerable problems to find employment. This is both due to a general skills mismatch between the young applicants, who have little practical experience or soft skills, and the jobs that are advertised, and because open positions might not always be advertised where young people look for them (e.g. on online platforms). As a result, it took young Italians, on average, a whopping 70.5 months (close to six years) to transition from school to permanent employment in 2000 (Pastore, 2012).

Worryingly, many young Italians who fail to find a job do not take up alternative tasks. Nearly 30% of all young Italians between 20 and 34 are NEET, and although not in education, employment, or training, they refrain from actively looking for a job. Italy's NEET ratio surpasses all other EU countries for both men and women and is considerably higher not only than the EU average (17.6%) but also other countries with a slack labour market, such as Spain (Eurostat, 2021b). While the percentage of NEETs is high even among university graduates (20%), the problem is especially pronounced among those who did not finish secondary education: 50% of youngsters with only primary or lower secondary education belong to the discouraged NEET group. With millions of parents who are supportive of letting their adult children live at home without contributing financially, hundreds of thousands of young Italians see little pressure to seek employment or to continue training or education, which aggravates Italy's already high NEET figures.

While youth unemployment among unskilled workers is considerably higher than that of their skilled peers, the number of people with a tertiary degree who are neither employed nor looking for a job also deserves special attention. Despite having completed their degree, about 11.3% of Italians aged 25 to 34 were unable to find a job (Statista (2021h). In addition, another 20% of Italians aged 20 to 34 with university degree were NEET, which means that nearly one in three young university graduates was economically inactive, despite not being in education or training. While this figure is worrisome on its own, the fact that Italy–next to Romania–has the lowest rate of university graduates aged 30 to 34 among all EU member states means that the Italian labour market is missing qualified people with tertiary education who can foster innovation and increase productivity.

Why are so many Italians not part of the labour force, despite having completed tertiary education? Similar to Italy's primary and secondary education, universities often fail to equip students with the skills demanded (and needed) by the corporate world. University degrees often provide in-depth theoretical knowledge while putting little focus on practical skills, experience, and soft skills. There are many arguments that point out that universities often do not prepare students for work life and that they do not offer enough support for job hunting and the transition between studies and employment. In contrast to other EU-15 countries, many Italians graduate from university without having done internships or experience staying abroad. Some graduates might not even have any work experience at all because student part-time jobs are not the norm, unlike in many other EU-15 countries, and living with their parents often removes the need to make their own money while studying. As a result, many Italians leave university with detailed theoretical knowledge, but without a clear idea about what they want to do for a living and about how to find a job–in addition to a lack of hands-on experience in their profession. Another reason for the relatively high youth unemployment among university graduates is the mismatch of qualifications and expertise needed in the labour market and the degrees pursued by students. The Italian labour market has a significant shortage of people trained in STEM (science, technology, engineering, and mathematics) subjects, but the majority of students enrol in humanities and social science degrees. As is true in most countries, it is harder to find jobs with these degrees.

The reason for the high rate of cohabitation among young Italians is, however, not only the lack of paid employment. Also the fact that Italians spend many years at university and graduate later than their peers in other EU member states prolongs their stay in the parental home. On average, in 2004, Italian students graduated from their first-level degree (such as a BA or BSc) when they were 25.5, and from their second-level degree (MA or MSc) aged 27.8 (and age 26.3 in 2013) (Cammelli/Gasperoni, 2015). One reason for this relatively high age of university graduates is that a considerable number of students change degree courses, which prolongs their stay at university. As a result, in 2004, only 15% of all students graduated withing the prescribed timeframe–a trend which has been considerable alleviated by the Bologna Process.

Italy's relatively high rate of school and university dropouts–about 13% of Italians aged 18–24 left education or training early–adds to the rise of accordion families, as leaving education without a degree makes the transition to paid employment more difficult (Statista, 2021d).

While the aforementioned factors pose valid points, it would be too simplistic to look for the reasons for Italy's high youth unemployment just among the 'supply side'–the youth. The labour market itself offers very little to younger workers. Due to Italy's long economic recessions over the past decades, and the slow economic growth since the introduction of the euro in 2001, job growth in Italy has been sluggish. This, combined with the rise of the retirement age in 2012, has led to fewer jobs being available to younger workers. As people now have to work until they turn 67, there are fewer job vacancies from the soon-to-be-retired workers that could be filled with by young generation in the past year.

Much of Italy's youth unemployment is structural. In 2014, over half of the 44% of young Italians out of work had been so for over a year. This shows that the country's high youth unemployment rate is part of a bigger problem and results from decades of low economic performance. Italy as a whole has suffered from a broad labour underutilisation. In fact, Italy's lack of utilisation of their labour force was at the very bottom, next to Greece, with about 42.9% of Italians not in education or training being either inactive, unemployed, or involuntarily in part-time jobs. Among 15–24-year-old part-time workers, an astonishing 83.7% were originally looking for a full-time position and settled for part-time involuntarily (Eurostat, 2022d). This high figure clearly shows that the underutilisation of young labour is often the result of a slack labour market and a decline of full-time positions over the previous decades. In fact, statistics revealed that, between 2000 and 2015, the number of 15–24-year-olds in full-time positions decreased from nearly 1,600,000 to 676,000 in 2015, marking a decline of nearly 60%. At the same time, the number of people in that age bracket working part-time increased by nearly 40% (OECD Stat, n.d.).

Government policies have shown little success in generating employment among all age and population groups in Italy, illustrating that it is, to a certain extent, the tight labour market itself and not only a lack of qualifications and experience among the young generation that is responsible for the country's low youth employment rate. The deregulation of the labour market and of working contracts in the 1990s contributed to the country's high youth unemployment, as it created a dual labour market where older workers were on well-paid permanent contracts, while younger workers could often only secure temporary positions. The prevalence of temporary contracts among younger workers means that in a recession, they can be made redundant quite easily. In many Italian companies, the discrepancies among older and younger workers have grown rapidly, with substantial gaps in employment protection and wages. As indefinite employment contracts are becoming increasingly rare, many young workers have become trapped in a series of unpaid or low-paid internships or in short-term contracts.

This leads us to the next reason for the long cohabitation among parents and children: a personal income too low for young adults to be able to afford their own housing. Italy has a one of the highest low-income rates among all OECD countries. About one in seven (14.7%) of all working-age Italians lived on less than 50% of the median equivalised household disposable income in 2015 (OECD, 2018a). This is especially prevalent in Italy's south, where wages are considerably lower than in the north. In Basilicata, for example, the average annual gross salary was below $24,500 in 2020–around 20% lower than in several northern regions (Statista, 2022). The south also has the highest percentage of low paid employees: at 17.4%, the rate of employees making less than two thirds of the country's median salary was over 2.5 times higher than in the northern regions (6.7%) (Statista, 2022).

A stark difference in income does not only exist between the different regions but also between different age groups. Poverty among young people–both employed and outside the labour market–is significantly higher because wages tend to rise with age and experience. Many younger workers start on very low salaries, also due to the temporary nature of their contracts. According to the 2016 Global 50 Remuneration Planning Report, Italy offered the lowest average compensation for full-time, entry-level jobs among all EU-15 countries. With an average gross salary of €27,400 p.a., Italian companies paid their new graduates not only 10% less than in the second worst performing country, Spain, but a whopping

€18,400 less than what Germans received for entry-level jobs (The Local, 2016). As rent in many Italian cities is high, the low wages for young employees make it very hard for adult children to move out of the parental home, even when working full-time (Statista, 2021b). Even if a young person manages to land a full-time entry-level job and gets paid just the national average for such a position, affording more than a 1–2-bedroom apartment is nearly impossible. Considering that a gross average salary of €27,400 p.a translates into take-home salary of €1,564 a month and that a one-room studio in Rome (which is only the 6th most expensive city in Italy) costs, on average, €663 per month, one can quickly see that the low starting salaries of most Italian employees make it difficult for young Italians to leave the family home, even if they want to (Statista, 2021g). A standard assumption is that a maximum of 30% of the income should be spent on rent (ideal rent-to-income ratio), which would mean that the average full-time employee in their first position has a mere €469 to spend on rent–a figure far too low to find any decent home in most Italian cities. In fact, close to 30% Italy's young adults aged 18-34 who live with their parents are in full-time positions (Eurostat, 2021a). Thus, it can be summarised that the low starting salaries–even for people with full-time positions–pose a major hurdle to residential independence.

The slack Italian labour market and the resulting high youth unemployment and prevalence of precarious work conditions among many young Italians on temporary contracts makes it difficult for hundreds of thousands to leave the parental home. With millions of Italian graduates being on short-term contracts or trapped in low-paid internships, many youngsters do not have the financial stability to look for an apartment and pay rent on their own. The unwillingness of many companies to hand out permanent contracts to young workers since the 1990s–by 2010, half of Italy's youth was on temporary contracts–, the many recessions, and the deep financial crisis Italy found itself after 2008 have aggravated the problem and increased many young Italians' dependence on their parents.

While the financial crisis of 2008 negatively impacted the financial situation of many youngsters in the EU, the Italian youth suffered disproportionately. Youth unemployment during the crisis was among the highest in the EU, meaning that young employees who lost their job often also had to give up their apartment and move back into the parental home. This was also the case because social security is lower in Italy than in most other EU-15 states, and because older workers receive considerably more generous welfare benefits than Italy's youth. Unemployment benefits are income-related, so the older, senior employees receive much larger amounts of benefits than new employees, and many occupational social welfare programmes are elderly-oriented. In fact, the most generous unemployment benefits–CIG (*cassa integrazione guadagni*) and *mobilità*–go to older workers. Up to today, many young workers under 30 receive little or no unemployment benefits at all. In fact, in 2016, nearly two thirds (61.1%) of 15–24-year-olds who registered as unemployed for six to eleven months received no benefits or assistance, which is also because unemployment benefits in Italy are dependent on the previous income (Eurostat, 2022b). This means that if a recent graduate failed to land a job, they would not qualify for unemployment benefits because they had not previously worked. The lack of own financial means and low state support for many young unemployed workers thus aggravate the housing issue.

The housing market

Italy's poor housing policies have led to high housing costs, which significantly impacts co-residence witnessed in Italian families. While the housing shortage in Italian cities is nowhere near as significant as it is in many other European cities, such as Berlin, Dublin, or London, it is often not an easy task for Italian youngsters to find affordable housing. This is because, historically, European cities were not built to host single households. Thus, only a fraction of the apartments on the market are small enough for youngsters being able to afford them. This is in contrast to Japan: while family-sized apartments are the exception rather than the norm on the Japanese rental market, Italy's housing stock in the cities mostly consists of 3–5-bedroom apartment. Although family fragmentation and the rise of nuclear families in many European cities has increased the demand for 1–2-bedroom flats, these are often not widely available, as housing is used for much longer in Italy than in Japan. In other words, with much of Italy's housing being built in the 19th or early 20th century, or at least 40–50 years ago, when one-bedroom flats were not common, small-sized housing is still an exception. If available, most 1–2-bedroom apartments tend to be modern and thus relatively expensive. As a result, young Italians with a low income who would like to move out of the parental home, but do not wish to share an apartment with others (a relatively common practice among students in European cities), find it difficult to find a suitable alternative to their childhood bedroom.

While starting salaries tend to be low in Italy, rents are not. Although rent levels are still significantly lower than in London, Stockholm or Paris, for example, the average rent surpasses €11 per square meter in six Italian regions (Statista, 2021c). This means that even if young Italians have a full-time job and are paid the average salary for entry-level positions, payments for rent would take up an unsustainable share of their take-home salary. The lack of affordable small studios for young Italians thus also contributes to the rise of accordion families, as many parents are against making their children move to a low-quality dwelling they could afford on their own.

Social factors

Not everything can be explained from a purely financial perspective. In fact, in many cases, both Italian youngsters and their parents prefer cohabitation. In the following, we will look at how social factors impact Italy's widespread cohabitation, such as altruism among Italian mothers, who enjoy taking care of their sons well into adulthood, a higher degree of dependence among many young male Italians, and the belief that the oldest son in particular should be pampered because he will continue the family line.

In Italy, the mother–*la mamma*–has had a strong impact on the family for centuries. Common clichés that Italian mothers love cooking for their family and pamper the whole extended family with scrumptious meals exist for a reason. *La mamma* typically means a housewife who devotes her life to making her children and husband happy, often by means of providing good food or pampering them emotionally. While Italian families have shrunk considerably due to the unprecedented low Italian birth rate over recent decades, the cliché of many Italian mothers being devoted housewives and cooks remains valid. In fact, Italy has the second lowest female employment rate in the whole of the EU. Despite the rising labour force participation of Italian women, nearly half of all women aged 20-64 were not in employment in 2018 (Eurostat, 2020b). To put this into perspective: on average, over two thirds of all working-age women (20–64) work in the EU, and in some countries, their share is as high as 80% (e.g. Sweden). Even in Japan, another country that historically had low inclusion of females in the labour market, the employment rate of women aged 15 to 64 now surpasses 72%.

The high prevalence of stay-at-home mothers in Italy often translates into many being in no rush for their children to leave the parental home. In fact, while in most countries surveyed, happiness among mothers increases with the departure of their children from the parental home, Italian mothers report a higher degree of happiness if their (adult) children are around (Tosi, 2017). This can be explained by the fact that for many Italian mothers, their lives (and purpose) centre on their children; many fall into a hole when their children move out, leaving them without a clear reason for being at home and for running the household. With Italian mothers historically leaving the labour market for marriage and childbirth and not returning afterwards, many enjoy having their adult children reside at home so they not only have someone to care (and cook) for but also have company during the day, when the husband is at work. Several studies support this view and suggest that parents living with their adult children derive some 'utility' from cohabitation. Mothers do the bulk of household chores for their children, but there is an expected role reversal when the parents reach old age and need support with tasks they are physically not comfortable with anymore (e.g. cutting trees, shovelling snow, and carrying heavy items). In addition, adult children often provide companionship and a different perspective on things, and give a continued purpose for many stay-at-home mothers. Even their conforming to household rules and parental regulations could make parents feel better. As a result, Tosi (2017) suggests that parents even derive some heath benefit from cohabitation, as they tend to be happier, healthier, and stronger when they live with their adult children. Parents' agreement with (or even liking of) cohabitation with their adult children can be seen by the fact that the commonly-used term for sons who do not leave the nest, *mammoni*, does not have a negative connotation. While some politicians, such as ex-finance minister Tomasso Padoa-Schiopa, derogatively referred to the mummy's boys as '*bamboccioni*' (big babies), the term *mammoni* is more neutral, This stands in stark contrast to Japan, where the term 'parasite single' implies a strong disrespect for those children who stay at home and 'live off' their parents.

However, it is not only the mothers or parents who derive utility from cohabitation. Newman (2012) has shown that over 40% of all *mammoni* stay at home with their parents because they enjoy the comforts of being housed and fed without having personal responsibilities. In many cases, Italian mothers cook for their sons (or daughters), wash and fold their laundry, clean their rooms (in addition to the rest of the apartment or house), do the groceries, take care of the garden (if applicable), pay the bills, and take care of all unforeseen incidents and problems. Parents often let their children use their car or pay for their private consumption. In other words, many children enjoy a better and more far-reaching service at 'Hotel Mamma' than any 5-star hotel could offer–and the service comes without a hefty bill at the end of the month. Thus, many Italian youngsters prefer cohabitation over residential independence because it not only lowers their expenditure, thus allowing them to spend more on personal consumption, but also because they enjoy being pampered and cared for while not having to shoulder much burden and responsibility.

Sociologists and anthropologists point to another factor for Italy's high cohabitation rate. Historically, families were dependent on their children, especially the first-born son, for old-age care. As Italy did not have a strong welfare state until recently and still puts a lot of emphasis on family ties, sons were not only expected to continue the family line and maintain its honourable reputation but also to secure their parents a comfortable life when their age impacts their ability to live independently. Thus, many Italian families pampers their sons, especially the first-born, and try to keep them close to the parental home to ensure that they are willing to care for parents at a later stage.

Another explanation for rise of accordion families is the widespread existence of family businesses where parents and children work next to each other. There are close to 800,000 family businesses in Italy, constituting over 85% of the total number of corporations in the country (AIDAF, n.d.). While such a high prevalence of family firms also exists in other EU countries, Italian family companies are different in terms of management, with two thirds of them being fully managed by family members. This stands in stark contrast to the UK, for example, where the share of family managed businesses without external managers is a mere 10%. In other words, many Italian family businesses are still run by the core family and in many cases, the son(s) (or daughters) work next to the father or grandfather, which often increases the attachment between the children and their parents and their willingness to cohabitate. Thus, it can be argued that the high prevalence of family firms, where several generations work and manage the business together is a further factor that increases residential independence of young Italians, as many families believe it is beneficial for the company if the family members live together and share their ideas and thoughts at the end of the workday. This also continues if the fathers retire or pass away, It can be concluded that Italy's high prevalence of family companies with father and son working together, or the sons taking over the business from the parents is another factor that explains the high cohabitation rate of adult children and their parents in Italy.

Several pull-factors, which in the past fostered or expedited the departure from the parental home, have now lost some of their power. In previous decades, having a life partner and wanting to live together was a major reason for children leaving the parental home. Yet, in recent years, many Italian youngsters seem to be less interested in finding a romantic partner and starting a family.

In 2019, the average age for Italian men to get married (the first time) was 35.5 years, making them the 4th oldest in the EU (Statista, 2021f). In some regions, such as Liguria, the average age at men's first marriage was as high as 38 years. While women tend to marry slightly earlier, they were, on average, also 32.7 years when they first tied the knot (Statista, 2021a).

While there is no doubt that the marriage age has risen sharply in Italy, there is considerable disagreement over whether this is due to the rise of *mammoni* and prolonged cohabitation between parents and sons. Some argue that delayed marriage is the result of fewer Italians having their own apartment, as this often impedes romantic relationships and family planning. However, others propose the opposite, claiming that because Italian youngsters find it increasingly hard to find a partner for life in times of 'loose' online dating and increasing gender equality, they opt to stay at home longer, enjoying the comfort of having companionship from their parents. Most academics, however, advocate that prolonged cohabitation poses a reason for (and not a result of) Italy's late marriage age and the country's low birth rate. Similarly, also representatives from the catholic church argued that cohabitation among adult children and their mothers put a risk to marriage and reduces the country's fertility rate. While it is true that Italy, at 3.1 marriages per 1,000 people p.a. (2019), has one of the lowest crude marriage rates in the EU, there are no studies that show a clear causality between prolonged cohabitation and low marriage rates. The fact that the crude marriage rate fell from 4.2 in 2008 to 3.2 in just ten years could also be the result of a rise of civil unions, people in relationships opting not to marry, and Italians not finding a suitable partner for other reasons (Statista, 2021e).

Conclusion

Do most of Italy's *mammoni* reside with their parents voluntarily because they want to enjoy the comforts of Hotel Mamma well into adulthood, or involuntarily because their financial situation does not allow them to rent an apartment on their own? This was one of the big questions that came up when trying to outline the reasons why so many Italian adult sons still live with their parents. The answer is both. While financial pressure due to spiralling youth unemployment after 2008, a high share of NEETs among Italy's youth, the prevalence of young employees in temporary and/or part-time positions, and high rents all pose significant reasons for delayed departure, financial reasons alone are insufficient to explain why the average age of Italian men leaving the parental home has surpassed 30 years and why only around a quarter of all Italian males aged 18 to 34 have residential independence. It is also the tight rental market, with its low availably of affordable housing for singles, that contributes to many youngsters being unable to move out of their childhood bedroom. Unlike in many other countries, cohabitation of parents and their adult children is, however, often not involuntary. Many Italian youngsters enjoy a better relationship with their parents than their peers in other countries and often opt to stay at home to benefit from the all-encompassing service their parents provide. Many Italian mothers, who have been stay-at-home mums and housewives for decades, do not mind pampering their adult children, reporting to gain. Several studies have suggested that Italian parents even derive some utility from the prolonged cohabitation with their children, as living together makes them happier than parents in many other countries (Mencari et al., 2020). The high prevalence of family-run business, with fathers and sons working next to each other (or with the children taking over from the parents), is a further factor that increases cohabitation, as many families consider it to be beneficial for the company if the children remain close to them.

Even if not all parents are happy with their adult children not leaving the nest, many prefer them to stay in the parental home than having to work long hours just to pay the bills for their own apartment. Yet, as full-time, permanent employment has become the exception rather than the norm for Italy's youth, mainly due to the deregulation of the labour market in the 1990s and the rise of a parallel economy with much less generous social protection and lower wages, many discouraged *mammoni* opt to become NEET than to proactively seek employment.

Italy's high share of youngsters that are not in employment, education, and training, nor actively looking for a job, could pose a serious danger for Italy's future. It cannot be denied that Italy's rise of accordion families potentially has far-reaching economic consequences. First of all, there is a well-grounded fear that late residential independence could delay marriage and reduce Italy's already low fertility even further. Second, with Italian youngsters after not feeling strong pressure to find a job by any means because they can live at home, supported by their parents, could contribute to the country's sluggish economy. In fact, Italy's slow economic growth over several decades can be attributed to the county's low employment rate, especially among women and the elderly. With many women and people over 55 being economically inactive, productivity and economic growth in Italy has historically been far below its EU-15 neighbours. This is because having fewer people in employment reduces the country's economic output and leads to lower aggregate demand (as the lack of income inhibits spending), while at the same time increases welfare spending by the government. Thus, having a big share of its youth not being part of the labour force could translate into lower economic output and a lower aggregate demand for goods while potentially contributing to long-term unemployment. The longer a young person is out of the labour market (or failed to enter it), the higher the chances that they will remain unemployed for years. Thus, it can be concluded that while prolonged cohabitation brings several benefits for the child, the parents and the Italian government, the dangers for the economy, but also for the young individuals themselves could potentially be large. Italy thus would be well-advised to combat long-term unemployment and the high NEET rate among youngsters to help them gain residential independency.

References

AIDAF (n.d.) *Family businesses in Italy.* Retrieved from
https://www.aidaf.it/en/aidaf-3/1650-2/

Destatis (n.d.). *December 2021: EU unemployment rate at 6.4%.* Retrieved from
https://www.destatis.de/Europa/EN/Topic/Population-Labour-Social-Issues/
Labour-market/EULabourMarketCrisis.html#:~:text=The%20youth%20
unemployment%20rate%20was,%25)%20and%20Italy%20(26.8%25)

Cammelli, A., and Gasperoni, G. (2015). *16th Almalaurea report on Italian University graduates' profile: Opportunities and challenges for higher education in Italy.* Almalaurea Working Papers 74. Retrieved from
https://www2.almalaurea.it/universita/pubblicazioni/wp/pdf/wp74.pdf

Eurostat (2019). *When are they ready to leave the nest?* Retrieved from
https://ec.europa.eu/eurostat/web/products-eurostat-news/-/EDN-20190514-1

Eurostat (2020a). *When are they ready to leave the nest?* Retrieved from
https://ec.europa.eu/eurostat/web/products-eurostat-news/-/edn-20200812-1

Eurostat (2020b). *Women's employment in the EU.* Retrieved from
https://ec.europa.eu/eurostat/de/web/products-eurostat-news/-/EDN-
20200306-1

Eurostat (2021a). *Living conditions in Europe - labour conditions.* Retrieved from
https://ec.europa.eu/eurostat/statistics-explained/index.php?title=Living_
conditions_in_Europe_-_labour_conditions#Young_adults_still_living_at_
home

Eurostat (2021b). *Statistics on young people neither in employment nor in education or training.* Retrieved from
https://ec.europa.eu/eurostat/statistics-explained/index.php?title=Statistics_
on_young_people_neither_in_employment_nor_in_education_or_training

Eurostat (2022a). *Involuntary part-time employment as percentage of the total part-time employment, by sex and age (%).* Retrieved from
https://appsso.eurostat.ec.europa.eu/nui/submitViewTableAction.do

Eurostat (2022b). *Unemployment by sex, age, duration of unemployment and distinction registration/benefits (%).* Retrieved from
http://appsso.eurostat.ec.europa.eu/nui/submitViewTableAction.do.

Liotti, G. (2020). Labour market flexibility, economic crisis and youth unemployment in Italy. *Structural Change and Economic Dynamics,* 54, 150–162

Manacorda, M., & Moretti, E. (2006). Why do Most Italian Youths Live with Their Parents? Intergenerational Transfers and Household Structure. *Journal of the European Economic Association,* 4 (4), 800–829

Mencarini, L., Pailhé, A., Solaz, A., and Tanturri, M.-L. (2017). The time benefits of young adult home stayers in France and Italy: a new perspective on the transition to adulthood? *Genus* 73 (60), 1–22.

OECD (2018a). *Good jobs for all in a changing world of work: The OECD jobs strategy.* Paris: OECD Publishing. Partially retrieved from
https://www.oecd.org/italy/jobs-strategy-ITALY-EN.pdf

OECD (2018b). *PISA 2015. Results in focus.* Retrieved from
https://www.oecd.org/pisa/pisa-2015-results-in-focus.pdf

OECD.Stat (n.d.). *FTPT employment based on a common definition.* Retrieved from https://stats.oecd.org/Index.aspx?DataSetCode=FTPTC_D

Pastore, F. (2012). *Youth unemployment in Italy at the time of the New Great Depression.* Berlin: Friedrich Ebert Foundation

Statista (2021a). *Average age of men at first marriage in Italy in 2019, by region.* Retrieved from https://www.statista.com/statistics/569603/men-average-age-at-first-marriage-in-italy-by-region/

Statista (2021b). *Average monthly rent of furnished dwellings in Rome in 2018, by number of rooms (in euros).* Retrieved from https://www.statista.com/statistics/1014548/average-monthly-rent-of-furnished-dwellings-in-rome-italy-by-number-of-rooms/#:~:text=According%20to%20the%20data%2C%20in,1.2%20thousand%20euros%20per%20month

Statista (2021c). *Average monthly rental price for residential properties in Italy as of August 2021, by region (in euros per square meter).* Retrieved from https://www.statista.com/statistics/818778/average-monthly-price-for-properties-for-rent-by-region-in-italy/

Statista (2021d). *Early leavers from education and training.* Retrieved from https://ec.europa.eu/eurostat/statistics-explained/index.php?title=Early_leavers_from_education_and_training

Statista (2021e). *Marriage rate in Italy from 2002 to 2020 (per 1,000 inhabitants).* Retrieved from https://www.statista.com/statistics/568092/marriage-rate-in-italy/

Statista (2021f). *Mean age at first marriage in selected European countries in 2019 by country and gender.* Retrieved from https://www.statista.com/statistics/612174/mean-age-at-first-marriage-in-european-countries/

Statista (2021g). *Monthly rental price per square meter in selected cities in Italy as of April 2021, by city (in euros per square meter).* Retrieved from https://www.statista.com/statistics/984515/italy-cities-with-the-highest-rent-for-a-dwelling/

Statista (2021h). *Unemployment rate among individuals aged 25 to 34 years in Italy as of 2020, by educational level.* Retrieved from https://www.statista.com/statistics/1108426/young-unemployed-people-by-educational-level-in-italy/

Statista (2021i). *Youth unemployment rate in Italy in 2020, by region.* Retrieved from https://www.statista.com/statistics/777086/youth-unemployment-rate-in-italy-by-region/

Statista (2022). *Average annual gross salary in Italy in 2020, by region.* Retrieved from https://www.statista.com/statistics/708972/average-annual-nominal-wages-of-employees-italy-by-region/

The Local (2016). Young Italian workers are among worst paid in Europe. *The Local*, 17 February 2016. Retrieved from https://www.thelocal.it/20160217/young-italian-workers-are-among-the-worst-paid-in-europe/

Tosi, M. (2017). "Age norms, family relationships, and home-leaving in Italy." *Demographic Research*, 36, 281–306

【著者略歴】

アンナ・シュラーデ（Anna Schrade）

関西学院大学産業研究所准教授

バース大学、パリ政治学院で修士号（MA in European Studies）、オックスフォード大学で修士号（MSc in Japanese Studies）と博士号（PhD in History）を取得。神戸大学で准教授として EU エキスパート人材養成プログラムを担当し、2018 年 4 月より現職。2019 年から 2022 年、関西学院大学が採択された欧州委員会のジャン・モネ・モジュールのリーダーを務める。

専門は EU と日本の政策比較。主に農村開発と労働移動を研究しており、幅広く発表活動を行っている。

A journey through Europe
Societies, politics, and contemporary issues in the EU

2022 年 8 月 31 日初版第一刷発行

著　者　Anna Schrade

発行者　田村和彦
発行所　関西学院大学出版会
所在地　〒 662-0891
　　　　兵庫県西宮市上ケ原一番町 1-155
電　話　0798-53-7002

印　刷　大和出版印刷株式会社